HOLINESS

Living Leaven Free

A little leaven leaveneth the whole lump.
(Galatians 5:9)

HOLINESS

Living Leaven Free

A little leaven leaveneth the whole lump.
(Gulutians 5:9)

by

PASTOR ROD PARSLEY

Columbus, Ohio
U.S.A.

DEDICATION

I thank God for my parents who trained me in the things of God.

In the early days of World Harvest Church, they enabled me to concentrate on my studies in Bible college, building the church and the things of God. They stood by me then, and they stand by me in ministry today.

I have never and will never stand by a man greater than my father. Some of the most powerful experiences I remember are those times when I was a child. My father would gather us in the living room. I can still hear him saying, "God, this is my family. And God, we need you. We need you in our family. We're not going to let the devil have our family."

My mother's lifestyle set a standard for me that I could never get away from. From her I learned respect for the Word of God. Her passion and determination became patterns for my life.

She is a praying mother. I still recall at eight years of age hearing her weeping in her prayer closet, saying, "God, please save my children." God heard her prayers then — and He hears her prayers now.

I lovingly dedicate this book to my parents.

I honor my father, James Parsley.

I honor my mother, Ellen Parsley.

As they serve God today, they are at my side in ministry. I trust their Godly counsel. In them the Scripture is fulfilled, *If therefore ye have not been faithful in the unrighteous mammon, who will commit to your trust the true riches? (Luke 16:11).*

TABLE OF CONTENTS

INTRODUCTION ———————————————— *11*

CHAPTER ONE
THE CORROSIVE EFFECTS OF LEAVEN ——— *34*

CHAPTER TWO
THE LEAVEN OF THE PHARISEES ———— *54*

CHAPTER THREE
THE LEAVEN OF THE SADDUCEES ———— *86*

CHAPTER FOUR
THE LEAVEN OF THE HERODIANS ———— *124*

CHAPTER FIVE
THE LEAVEN OF THE CORINTHIANS ——— *148*

CHAPTER SIX
THE LEAVEN OF THE GALATIANS ———— *180*

CHAPTER SEVEN
THE CLEANSING SOLUTION ——————— *214*

One Drop Of Water

A single drop of water fell gently, unnoticed, onto the iron support beam of one of the largest bridges in America.

Day by day, other droplets followed, silently but surely landing on that same beam. Without anyone taking particular notice, the drops of water began a corrosive chemical reaction with the iron, forming a brittle, reddish coating on the beam.

The moist air continued to deposit drops of water.

Because the majestic bridge was so cosmetically beautiful, gleaming brightly in the sun, no one noticed the drops or the tiny reddish brown spots as they formed on the smooth surface of the sturdy iron beam.

Rust formed and spread without interference.

Week by week, month by month, year by year, bit by bit, the spots of rust spread. As they grew, they ever-so-gently sapped the tensile strength from that huge, sturdy chunk of iron.

If the rust had been found and dealt with soon enough, there might not have been a problem.

But, the rust was ignored ... left alone to eat away at the iron beam.

Over the years, the very integrity of the main support beam of the bridge was compromised. The rust, free to reap its corrosive effect, kept eating away at the iron until first it penetrated the surface, and then eventually, the very core of the beam.

One day, suddenly, unexpectedly, the bridge collapsed, killing everyone on it.

Another drop of water falls on the rubble and ruin that was once the majestic bridge ... and the corrosion continues.

INTRODUCTION

SPIRITUAL AIDS RAVISHES
THE UNSUSPECTING CHURCH

What a sense of joy and anticipation I felt in my heart as I held the first, long-awaited copy of *Repairers of the Breach* in my hands.

For one full year I had lived with that god-given message.

Preaching it.

Rejoicing in it.

Taking it deeper into my spirit.

God commissioned me to commit that revelation to print, and on that exciting day in 1992 that message at last materialized into the volume I was now holding in my hands.

I felt satisfied in what I thought was the completion of the task the Lord had set before me, and rejoiced at the realization of how many lives God would forever change through these foundational spiritual truths.

But God cut short my time of celebration.

"You're not finished yet," He told me in the midst of my rejoicing.

"What do you mean, Lord?" I respectfully asked, somewhat surprised.

"You've only delivered the first half of that message," He said.

11

Repairers of the Breach was birthed from Isaiah 58:12, *And thou shalt be called, The repairer of the breach, The restorer of paths to dwell in.*

Man committed sin — high treason against God — and fell in the Garden of Eden. That sin opened a breach — a chasm between God and man. Suffering, crying humanity desperately needed a way to bridge that chasm and experience, once again, the life-giving reality of God.

From the moment of the fall, God lovingly began to build a bridge to "repair the breach," to bring mankind back into a place of intimate fellowship with Him.

God stuck a cross in the middle of that chasm, and hung His Son on it. He shed the sinless blood of a crucified Carpenter from Nazareth on that bridge so the devil could not cross, and so we could be saved.

He bridged that chasm and suffered so that *with his stripes we are healed (Isaiah 53:5),* no longer having to be victims of cancer, heart attacks or AIDS.

Jesus is the bridge between man and God.

He pushed back the forces of darkness from that Gospel bridge and then gave us the foundational, biblical planks of power to keep it strong.

Jesus delivered us from the shackles and chains of bondage, and gave us freedom through that deliverance to function victoriously in every area of our lives.

God sent His Lamb, pure and spotless, so that we, too, might be made holy.

In *Repairers of the Breach* I shared seven foundational biblical truths, vital planks in the Gospel bridge, that
had been stolen by the devil. God showed me how to
secure each plank on that Gospel bridge — an uncrossable
bridge for man alone, but crossable now through the blood
of Jesus.

Today, Jesus sits at the right hand of the Father to
bring us from where we are to where we can be, to bring
us from sorrow to success, from poverty to prosperity,
from the gutter to glory, from victim to victory, from hell
to heaven.

In *Repairers of the Breach,* I shared how the devil
invaded the Church and blatantly stole our Gospel truths.
He robbed us of the doctrine of salvation by the blood of
the Lamb — so we secured that biblical plank firmly in
the bridge.

He robbed the Church of the baptism in the Holy
Spirit, but we also restored that foundational plank to the
bridge.

One by one, we restored the planks.

"Lord, I have painstakingly exposed what Satan has
stolen from the Church. What do you want me to do
now?" I asked, eager to know where the Lord was leading me.

"Read the verse again," I heard in my spirit.

So I did.

13

*And thou shalt be called, The repairer of
the breach, The restorer of paths to dwell in
(Isaiah 58:12).*

Then God began to reveal to me the truths contained within these pages.

Repairers of the Breach awakened the Church to what has been stolen by the devil, and instructed the body of Christ how to put it back.

But repair is far different from total and complete restoration!

Repairers of the Breach mustered some of the troops. We have strapped on the holy armor of God. Our feet have been shod with the preparation of the Gospel of peace. We have girded our loins about with truth, put on the breastplate of righteousness and the helmet of salvation. We have armed ourselves with the shield of faith and the sword of the Spirit *(Ephesians 6:11).*

Yes, the bridge has been repaired.

But the Church keeps allowing Satan to subtly chip away at the newly-installed Gospel planks on that bridge until they once again become weak.

We can repair a bridge with a new iron beam, but if we do not protect that beam, a small speck of rust, over time, will weaken that beam until one day it collapses, just like the one before it.

The process is slow.

At first, almost imperceptible.

God began to show me that the Church not only

needs to repair the gaps in the bridge with strong Gospel planks, but then it must learn how to recognize the subtle, corrosive attacks of the devil as he attempts to weaken that bridge.

Once and for all, the Church must assume its god-given position of authority over the powers of darkness and rebuke the devil from its midst.

Seduction is Subtle

Sex is portrayed in our movie theaters and on our television screens as a fun, exciting, seductive and spontaneous experience — with no negative repercussions.

The media message is that "Sex is a wonderful adventure. You should do it, whether you are married or not, whether you know the person or not, whether you are the same sex or not. Just do it now, and make it spontaneous! Fun! Wild! Kinky!"

Underneath the sexual hype there lives a killer reality that clearly thrives on these lies.

AIDS.

It is the deadliest contagious disease ever to hit this planet.

AIDS kills virtually everyone it infects.

In 1981, there were only 200 patients with AIDS.

Today, an estimated 240,000 AIDS-infected Americans are dead or dying.[1]

If the disease is so insidious, and so final, then why is it spreading?

Because no one REALLY believes the problem is THAT bad. Instead, we reassure each other that "Everything is going to be all right," or "It can't happen to me," or that somehow, some way, AIDS will go away — or a cure will soon be discovered "before I get it and die."

Teenagers tell themselves AIDS "only happens to homosexuals and drug addicts."

In the meantime, instead of hard and truthful answers, we hear simplistic solutions from supposedly knowledgeable sources.

"You don't have to stop having sex with multiple partners," the government tells us, "just practice SAFE SEX. Use a condom and enjoy yourself."

"If you are going to do drugs," the American Medical Association advises, "just make sure you use a clean needle to shoot up your heroin."

"AIDS can only be transferred by open cuts in the skin," the newspaper and communication media report, ignoring increasing medical evidence that, in some cases, it can actually be transmitted through the air and through the skin ... even without open cuts!

There are cases of AIDS now reported that do not fit any of the known ways to contract the disease. These victims have no known cause for their sickness, yet they are infected with the HIV virus.

The lies and deceptions of the devil allow the AIDS virus to continue to spread its insidious infection to ever-increasing numbers of unsuspecting victims who are misinformed and foolishly confident that death will never strike at their doorstep.

AIDS is so subtle!

The virus can appear to lie dormant and unnoticed for years, all the while continuing to spread its deadly infection.

The devil has deceived a whole generation, leading them into falsely believing sex before marriage is okay and sex with "just a few partners" is not really THAT bad. These deceptions have produced huge increases in many other sexually-transmitted diseases besides AIDS.

These other diseases, like herpes, are seldom mentioned anymore, but make no mistake about it — they were just the forerunners of the deadliest disease ever to hit the shores of America! They pale in the path of AIDS — a seemingly unstoppable disease that is eating away at our population.

Deadly Deceptions

When AIDS first appeared, we were told it was strictly a homosexual disease.[2]

That proved to be incorrect.

Then, we were told it could only be transmitted through blood transfusions ... not tiny cuts.

That information proved faulty.

When at least 100 health care workers became infected, the AIDS experts had to admit it could also be transmitted by specks of blood.[3]

Next, we were told AIDS could be spread through heterosexual sex — but only through an HIV strain isolated in Africa.

Today, heterosexual women in America are the fastest rising risk group for AIDS.

Next, we were told the HIV virus could only be contracted through breaks in the skin. Now, we are learning that while skin is a barrier, it is not a complete barrier.

The latest information on AIDS reveals...

The AIDS virus can survive freezing.

The AIDS virus does not die on contact with air.

The AIDS virus can live on a dried surface for seven days.[4]

The misinformation and deception continues while an entire generation is dying.

A carrier of the AIDS virus looks healthy, and can appear that way for many years. The virus appears to lie dormant, deceiving the carrier with the illusion of good health, while it slowly eats away at the body's defense mechanisms.

Then one day the disease is exposed, and the victim can virtually do only one thing — prepare for death.

Spiritual AIDS in the Church

Just as an insidious virus called AIDS is eating away at the physical fiber of this generation, there is an insidious parasite in the spiritual world that is destroying the moral fabric of our Church. It is the deadliest disease we have ever seen in spiritual history.

My son, attend to my words; incline thine ear unto my sayings. Let them not depart from thine eyes; keep them in the midst of thine heart. For they are life unto those that find them, and health to all their flesh. Keep thy heart with all diligence; for out of it are the issues of life (Proverbs 4:20-23).

God is telling us to keep our heart with diligence, to protect it from vile words. The word *keep* in this verse literally means to guard. We are to guard our heart and keep it as pure as a loving father would his virgin daughter.[5]

God showed me now that the seven Gospel planks have been put back in place on the Gospel bridge ... we MUST keep them from the eroding lies and deceptions of the enemy!

It is time to tell the devil to take his hands off our families and our lives!

It is time to proclaim to the devil, "This old Gospel bridge does not belong to you. We are fed up with you slipping in and eroding the strength of the body of Christ."

Satan has two predominant corrosive tactics he uses to corrupt the planks of the Gospel.

First, he is a thief.

The thief cometh not, but for to steal, and to kill, and to destroy: I am come that they might have life, and that they might have it more abundantly (John 10:10).

For Satan to steal, he does not have to be strong or flex mighty muscles.

All he needs to do is enter your home when you are gone ... when the house is left unprotected.

The thief enters without force when we fail to pray, when we continue to sin, when we straddle the fence between sanctification and sin, when we are not walking in the fullness of the power of God — filled with His Spirit.

The Church has not been zealously guarding the doctrines Christ placed in the Church to give it power!

We have failed to keep — like a father guarding his virgin daughter — the faith!

We have allowed the humanistic theologians to steal from our hearts and our services the soul-saving songs about the blood, the life-changing sermons about the Second Coming, the doctrine of sin, and the doctrine of eternal judgment.

We have not been home spiritually; we have left ourselves unprotected.

AIDS has spread so furtively we have not seen the danger, and we have not been vigilant to protect ourselves against it.

So the virus enters the body, apparently laying dormant for years, deceiving the carrier into believing he is in good health. Sex continues, and many others are infected with the same deadly disease.

Satan uses this same corrosive tactic to attack the sleeping Church.

The darkened mind of Lucifer deceives our un-protected Church into thinking everything is all right. "The services look good. The sound system is working. There was a good turnout at the last church picnic. We are on the right road."

The lie infecting the body of Christ says we are doing a great job — that eighty-eight percent of America is Christian.[6]

That is not the case.

It is a lie.

We have left our homes empty and unprotected, and spiritual AIDS is ravishing the body of Christ.

We congratulate ourselves on our marvelous music ministry, but fail to recognize that thirty-two percent of Christians believe adultery between consenting, married adults is totally acceptable!

We rejoice in the dedicated and select few attending the latest Bible study, but fail to recognize that sixty-three percent of ALL Christians in America cannot even name the four Gospels!

We applaud the concepts contained in the Ten Commandments, yet seventy-one percent of the American Church admits they expect to lie, cheat and steal in the future![7]

In *Repairers of the Breach,* I shared how to restore the paths to dwell in. We put back the planks on the Gospel bridge that the devil had blatantly stolen.

Now it is time to shine the light of the Gospel on

what we have given our lives to protect, into the darkness of the deception of the Antichrist that is lurking in the hearts of believers, and in the churches of America and around the world.

A far more insidious plan is underway than open thievery. The blighted mind of Satan has employed a diabolical scheme to deceive the Church into thinking everything is all right.

Everything is Not All Right!

There are people in the body of Christ who are mere shells of men.

Jude called them clouds without water.

Clouds they are without water, carried about of winds; trees whose fruit withereth, without fruit, twice dead, plucked up by the roots (Jude 12).

Paul said these hollow men, without any spiritual substance, were *as sounding brass, or a tinkling cymbal (1 Corinthians 13:1).*

Jesus was even more blunt in His assessment of these men and women who pretended to have a relationship with God:

Ye serpents, ye generation of vipers, how can ye escape the damnation of hell? (Matthew 23:33).

In Dante's inferno, the worst place in hell was reserved for the hypocrites, the men and women who looked beautiful on the outside, but were corrupt to the core in their hearts.[8]

Jesus hated the hypocrites who dressed in white, yet had corrosive leaven in their hearts:

Woe unto you, scribes and Pharisees, hypocrites! for ye are like unto whited sepulchres, which indeed appear beautiful outward, but are within full of dead men's bones, and of all uncleanness (Matthew 23:27).

God has shown me that many of the planks we have put back into our Gospel bridge appear stable, but are cracked and rotting underneath.

The devil has employed his deadly scheme of destruction, undermining and diluting the basic truths of the Gospel by sowing leaven into unleavened bread.

It is time to expose the devastating scheme of the devil; and once exposed, to take out the weakened planks and replace them with pure, unadulterated, foundational truths — to be kept solid and unblemished until Jesus comes!

There is an enemy within that is worse than AIDS, and it is eating away at the body of Christ.

Paul said, *A little leaven leaveneth the whole lump (Galatians 5:9).*

Leaven is spiritual AIDS.

It has no odor.

You cannot see it.

You cannot detect it with the senses.

Leaven works secretly, silently.

It does not walk up and say, "Hello, I am error in the Church, and I will lead you on a path of destruction and damn your soul to hell."

Leaven dresses itself in the trappings of religion.

It is time to announce the truth.

I would just as soon hold hands with a prostitute as a false prophet. I am tired of holding funerals for cancer patients and having a six-foot icicle declare that it was "God's will to pick another flower for heaven."

It is time to take back the Church!

To take back the pulpits!

To take back the airwaves!

The humanistic spirit the Church is courting, in the name of religion, is the demonic spirit of death.

Much of the Church is dressed in white flowing robes, but those long silk robes will never cover the rot and decay in their hearts.

Religious tradition that compromises the blood-bought Gospel is death.

The Church is being erroded by spiritual AIDS, and no one seems to notice or care.

"Christians should just respect other religions and not try to convert them to accept Jesus" is a lie that will bring certain damnation for unsaved millions.

Do you see it?

In the name of compromise, in the name of religion, in the name of humanistic theology, leaven is infecting the body of Christ, and it is polluting the whole loaf!

Satan does not have any new tricks. He is using the same tactics he has always used to dilute and destroy the truths of the Gospel bridge.

But God has revealed his deadly tactics in the Scriptures, if we will only take heed. He has laid before us in the New Testament five forms of leaven: the leaven of the Pharisees, the leaven of the Sadducees, the leaven of the Herodians, the leaven of the Corinthians, and the leaven of the Galatians.

It is imperative that the body of Christ learn how to discern, expose and eradicate each of these erosive elements.

Keep thy heart with all diligence; for out of it are the issues of life (Proverb 4:23).

The Road to Death!

The night before Ted Bundy was executed, I watched an interview with him and Dr. James Dobson on television. Bundy was a mass killer who heinously, viciously, violently, uncontrollably and demonically murdered, raped and ravaged many women.

Yet, according to various newspaper accounts, he was also an intelligent person with a brilliant mind and a pleasant personality — a handsome young man raised in a Christian home.

As that man sat handcuffed in his jail cell, the things he expressed to Dr. Dobson were insightful and frightening.

He told how he shuddered to think of the kind of people who are walking loose in our society in the 1990s — because our society has become so infested with pornography.

Bundy confessed that his road to sin started when "I found a few discarded magazines along the roadway. As a young boy, I began to feed myself on the images in those magazines, to fuel my thoughts, until they suddenly grasped hold of me and would not let go."

Now remember, Bundy was talking about twenty years ago when porn shops were hard to find; they were not on every corner of every major city like they are today. He could not view x-rated movies on television. He could not find pornography at the corner convenience store.

The virus entered his unprotected home, and eventually, his entire moral structure collapsed from the corrosive nature of sin!

He that believeth on me, as the scripture
hath said, out of his belly shall flow rivers of
living water (John 7:38).

The unleavened bread of the Gospel brings with it living water, but each particle of leaven pollutes the body of Christ. Like a land mine secretly planted in the dark of night, leaven remains hidden just below the surface until it is suddenly triggered into a spiritual explosion, ultimately blasting its victim with such destruction and devastation that there is nothing left but dust and death.

It is time to get the leaven out!

The Church looks healthy on the outside, but it is

full of dead men's bones.

God is calling the Church to resist the leaven, to tear it out of the body of Christ — no matter where we find it!

If leaven is in your church, get it out.

If leaven is in your life, pluck out the poison!

Root it out!

In this endtime hour, we must cleanse the Church of its debilitating leaven if the fruit of God is to flourish ... if we are to ignite the smoldering embers of revival.

Beware a Generalized Gospel!

God's way is narrow.

Because strait is the gate, and narrow is the way, which leadeth unto life, and few there be that find it (Matthew 7:14).

A generalized Gospel preaching an all-inclusive, non-condemning, watered-down version of Christianity will never save one solitary soul! It is time to return to the narrow way — to become a living remnant of the Church of Jesus Christ of Nazareth washed in the blood, bought with a price, redeemed from every nation, filled with the Holy Ghost, looking for the Second Coming, and operating in signs, wonders and apostolic authority!

Howbeit in vain do they worship me, teaching for doctrines the commandments of men. For laying aside the commandment of God, ye hold the tradition of men, as the washing of pots and cups: and many other such like things ye do (Mark 7:7,8).

It is time to expose the commandments of men. It is time to expose the lie that a little bit of compromise, to keep everyone happy, to not rock the boat ... will do no harm.

Our planks have been weakened!

Satan has sown leaven into unleavened truth. He has mixed tares with wheat.

And in the time of harvest I will say to the reapers, Gather ye together first the tares, and bind them in bundles to burn them: but gather the wheat into my barn (Matthew 13:30).

God says all leaven must be removed.

For whosoever eateth that which is leavened, even that soul shall be cut off from the congregation of Israel, whether he be a stranger, or born in the land. Ye shall eat nothing leavened; in all your habitations shall ye eat unleavened bread (Exodus 12:19,20).

The Church of Jesus Christ was born through men and women who did not know the meaning of compromise. Eleven of the twelve disciples were martyred for the conviction of their beliefs.

Recognize the Great Whore

The compromising, leaven-filled Church of today is drunken with the blood of the saints of God. It is time to search out and expose the masquerading church the book of Revelation calls the harlot church.

And there came one of the seven angels
which had the seven vials, and talked with me,
saying unto me, Come hither; I will show unto
thee the judgment of the great whore that sitteth
upon many waters (Revelation 17:1).

The great whore sits upon many waters. Those waters are representative of multiplied millions of human beings she will lure by her enticements to the very pit of hell. She sits in corrupt authority over them, holding them captive through their sins!

With whom the kings of the earth have
committed fornication, and the inhabitants of
the earth have been made drunk with the wine
of her fornication (Revelation 17:2).

The combination of government and religion is the most deadly combination and corrosive agent against revival we will ever see. Ultimately, government and man-made religion will unite in the final hours of the endtime, spiritual drama of the human family, and they alone will tower above and be the crown jewel of Satan's kingdom.

Be not deceived.

It is not God's intention to bring revival through government.

Some might say, "You must just mean communism or socialism."

No, I mean all of them!

God has one institution, and it is not in Washington, D.C., or in Rome, or in Moscow ... it is the Church!

Stop waiting for revival to come through governments; revival is coming through the Church. Revival is not coming through politicians, but through men and women who have sanctified and purified themselves at the altar of prayer.

Beware of governments and man-made religions uniting. They are made drunk with the blood of the saints of God.

It began that way.

It will end that way.

Get ready for it!

Get the leaven out.

If we are not willing to die for Christ, then we are in the wrong kingdom. Let the real Church of Jesus Christ stand up and become so strong that the pharaohs of our day say, "There are more of them than there are of us."

Let us show them that the more they persecute us, the more we prosper and grow, and the mightier we become! We thrive on their persecution.

Your faith groweth exceedingly, and the charity of every one of you all toward each other aboundeth; So that we ourselves glory in you in the churches of God for your patience and faith in all your persecutions and tribulations that ye endure (2 Thessalonians 1:3,4).

The harlot church is as deadly as the Antichrist spewing out his blasphemies.

So he carried me away in the spirit into the wilderness: and I saw a woman sit upon a scarlet coloured beast, full of names of blasphemy, having seven heads and ten horns.

And the woman was arrayed in purple and scarlet colour, and decked with gold and precious stones and pearls, having a golden cup in her hand full of abominations and filthiness of her fornication:

And upon her forehead was a name written, MYSTERY, BABYLON THE GREAT, THE MOTHER OF HARLOTS AND ABOMINATIONS OF THE EARTH.

And I saw the woman drunken with the blood of the saints, and with the blood of the martyrs of Jesus: and when I saw her, I wondered with great admiration (Revelation 17:3-6).

It is time to get the great whore out of the true Church and out of our lives! We must not allow this spirit in our hearts or in our churches.

The great whore encourages fornication and blasphemy. She is clothed in gold and precious stones, yet commits abominations and filthiness.

She is drunken with the blood of the saints, and it is time to kick her out of the Church once and for all. It is deadly to allow her polluting leaven.

I am tired of Christians remaining silent while prayer is yanked from our schools and our heritage.

I am fed up with so-called religious groups that invite conference speakers like Playboy Enterprises CEO Christie Hefner to speak on AIDS and other topics such as keeping lesbianism fun and same-sex sharing sessions.[8]

I am disgusted with harlot denominations who allow homosexual ministers to lead their flocks.

I am sickened with Christians who "lovingly" tell the non-Christians, "We are the same spirit" ... "God honors your heart" ... and "Even though you do not believe that Jesus Christ is Lord, we know we'll see you in heaven!"

It is time to get the leaven out and return to the blood-bought Gospel of Jesus Christ.

It is time to search out and destroy the great whore's rotten planks of religious traditionalism, fornication, and blasphemy, and restore the Gospel bridge with sturdy, incorruptible planks.

Do you want revival?

Will you give anything to receive it?

What if it means your life?

I would not give a penny for a religion that men were not willing to die for. I am not only talking about physical death; I am talking about social death.

Society will increasingly mock us as we protest the killing of innocent babies.

Reporters will continue to laugh at us in the national newspapers whenever there is scandal in the body of Christ, or whenever some person, in the name of God, kills someone.

Expect it.

To be the friend of the liberal, god-hating media in this generation is to be the enemy of the cross.

Our religious friends will shake their heads saying, "We do not understand you. We do not know what motivates you."

This religious crowd needs to search its hearts, cleanse its soul, and get the leaven out of the Church!

A little bit of leaven ruins the whole lump.

Just a little bit of it.

The faith of a mustard seed can move a mighty mountain, but a little leaven will ruin your whole heart, your whole mind, and your whole will.

Get the leaven out — today — while you still can!

CHAPTER ONE

THE CORROSIVE EFFECTS
OF LEAVEN

*Know ye not that a little leaven
leaveneth the whole lump?
(1 Corinthians 5:6)*

"Welcome to our forty-second monthly All Faith's Compromise meeting," said Farah See. "Today's meeting will be opened by Reverend Dee Lution.

"Thank you, Farah," the lesbian preacher said. "Let's pray. Oh, Heavenly Father or Mother, we thank you for blessing this meeting today. We ask you to draw us closer together to you, and to our families, however they are constituted. Help us eliminate the differences between Jews and Christians, and the prejudices against homosexuals and lesbians. We dedicate this meeting to all the suffering children in Somalia, and to a woman's right to choose. And, we pray these things in the precious name of Je ... ah, and we thank you, Lord. Amen."

"Dee, that was a real nice interdenominational prayer. Thank you. On today's agenda you will notice that our topic of discussion is 'What's all this fuss about being born-again, anyway?' We will begin this discussion with the rabbi who will explain why the born-again experience is not necessary to have a happy walk with God. Rabbi."

"Thank you, Farah," the rabbi replied, adjusting his microphone.

The thirty-four people at the meeting dutifully looked at their notes as the rabbi began to speak. One denominational minister over in the corner, reading ahead, had already circled two very important points:

1. Why Christ is not essential to heavenly living here on earth.
2. How Jews and Christians can worship together through two minor compromises.

Nodding in agreement to the insights in these notes, the denominational minister made a mental note to preach these two points at next Sunday's service.

THE CORROSIVE EFFECTS OF LEAVEN

It is time to WAKE UP and recognize what is going on in the Church!

The enemy just keeps gnawing away, deceiving us into accepting one theological lie after another, luring us into practicing a compromised Gospel, until the diluted body we call the Church is pleasingly palatable to everyone but God.

The Church has changed its dogmas and traditions so completely that now it rarely offends anyone who hears it — except God Himself.

Within the Church we have advocates for abortion, ministers who are gay, and people that do not pray.

The Bible does not say we should dilute the Gospel to please every little religious crowd.

The Bible does not say we should compromise for the sake of congeniality.

The Bible says,

> *I know thy works, that thou art neither cold nor hot: I would thou wert cold or hot. So then because thou art lukewarm, and neither cold nor hot, I will spew thee out of my mouth ... He that hath an ear, let him hear what the Spirit saith unto the churches (Revelation 3:15,16,22).*

It is time, once again, for the Church to show the people their transgressions and point out their sins. No one likes a message about sin, but it is the one thing we all have in common. It is the one thing that stops us from receiving all that God intends for us.

It is time for a change in our neighborhoods when teenagers run up and down our city streets with Uzi machine guns.

It is time for a change in our hearts when we rip 4,500 innocent lives out of the wombs of their mothers every day in this nation, then throw the corpses away in trash cans — or use them for scientific research.[1]

It is time for a change when a rock singer can strut across a stage and pronounce that the crucifixion is sexy because there is a naked man hanging on the cross.

It is time to get psychology out of our pulpits and put back the blood-bought Gospel of Jesus Christ.

It is time to get Christians out of their comfortable pews and into the unsaved streets, sharing the truth of Jesus Christ with their fellow workers, friends and neighbors.

Wake up!

Something is not working when divorce ravages Christian marriages just as easily as those in the secular world.

Something is not working when, in the most affluent nation on the face of this planet, men and women walk up and down the streets with no place to put their heads at night, no blanket to shield themselves from the cold, and no food to eat.

Something is not working when little children in this nation go to bed hurting, the abused victims of their own flesh and blood.

It is time to get the leaven out!

Leaven Pollutes and Taints

Leaven is the substance added to dough and liquids that causes fermentation, and in the Bible it always symbolizes sin. Unleavened bread symbolizes the absolute purity of God — without any contamination.

Spiritual leaven is anything in our life that saps spiritual strength, anything contrary to the Gospel, anything that comes against the life of God in the body of Christ.

Grain offerings presented to God by the Israelites were forbidden to be made with leaven.

No meat offering, which ye shall bring unto the Lord, shall be made with leaven: for ye shall burn no leaven, nor any honey, in any offering of the Lord made by fire (Leviticus 2:11).

During the Festival of Unfermented Cakes, which took place for seven days following the Passover celebration, nothing leavened was permitted in the Israelites' homes.

Seven days shall ye eat unleavened bread; even the first day ye shall put away leaven out of your houses: for whosoever eateth leavened bread from the first day until the seventh day,

39

that soul shall be cut off from Israel (Exodus 12:15).

The search to remove the leaven did not take place until AFTER the Passover — AFTER the blood had been applied that brought them from death to life!

In the Old Testament, the Israelite fathers thoroughly searched their homes, took all of the leaven out and burned it. The removal of the leaven symbolically separated them from the world.

But the Church has failed to persevere in its scriptural directive to keep itself clean from all forms of leaven. The five forms of leaven rampant in the Church today are producing the kingdom of hell in the body of Christ even AFTER they have been through the Passover!

Leaven, like rust when left unattended and blatantly ignored, becomes HIGHLY corrosive until it totally contaminates and destroys!

A little leaven spoils the whole lump.

The kingdom of heaven is like unto leaven, which a woman took, and hid in three measures of meal, till the whole was leavened (Matthew 13:33).

Leaven always pollutes the place it resides. One small bit of leaven can contaminate three measures of meal.

It is never good.

Jesus repeatedly warned His followers to watch out for leaven.

*Then Jesus said unto them, Take heed and
beware of the leaven of the Pharisees and of
the Sadducees (Matthew 16:6).*

When Jesus told His followers to beware of the
leaven, He was warning against the false doctrine and
hypocritical practices of His day, practices He knew had
a corrosive effect on the very souls of men.

Leaven has been associated with corruption down
through the ages. Plutarch, a Greek biographer, spoke of
it as "the product of corruption, and produces corruption
in the dough with which it is mixed."[2]

Leaven will lead us into the kingdom of darkness.

Without it, we can walk in the Kingdom of Light.

God is calling us to get the leaven out of our lives
and move on into the unleavened bread of holiness!

Leaven and Prayers Do Not Mix!

In one dramatic passage in the Bible, God rebukes
transgressing Israel with these words:

*And offer a sacrifice of thanksgiving
with leaven, and proclaim and publish the
free offerings: for this liketh you, O ye children
of Israel, saith the Lord God (Amos 4:5).*

God was telling the Israelites that all their worship
at Bethel and at Gilgal was transgression against Him, so
they might as well offer leavened or unleavened bread on
the altar.

Why?

41

Because all their offerings were already in vain ... they were committing idolatry. God was telling them, "As long as you are going to sin, you might as well offer me leavened sacrifices while you are at it, since I'm not going to honor what you do anyway."

When Jesus spotted leaven, He quickly came against it. He boldly denounced the leaven of the Pharisees, calling them hypocrites because they were more concerned with outward show than with the inner chambers of their hearts.

He pointed out the wrong doctrinal viewpoints of the Sadducees, declaring their rejection of the resurrection of man to be contrary to God's Word.

He exposed the immoral, lustful actions, the hypocrisy and the political treachery of the followers of Herod.

Paul rebuked the Galatians for foolishly seeking out their salvation through works, reminding them that they were not justified by the law, but by grace.

The church at Corinth was warned about the leaven of malice and wickedness.

Leaven permeates and corrupts whatever it comes in contact with, and God wants it purged from every crevice of our lives!

Purge out therefore the old leaven, that ye may be a new lump, as ye are unleavened. For even Christ our passover is sacrificed for us! Therefore let us keep the feast, not with old leaven, neither with the leaven of malice and wickedness; but with the unleavened bread of sincerity and truth (1 Corinthians 5:7,8).

Paul goes on to tell us not to mix with the fornicators of the world, or with the idolaters and extortioners. They will pollute our souls just as surely as a little leaven contaminates the entire loaf.

If any man that is called a brother be a fornicator, or covetous, or an idolater, or a railer, or a drunkard, or an extortioner; with such an one no not to eat (v.11).

It is time for the body of Christ to clear out the unclean, corrupting influence of immorality. Just as the Israelites would permit absolutely no leaven in their homes during the festival, God wants no leaven in our hearts.

Stand fast therefore in the liberty wherewith Christ hath made us free, and be not entangled again with the yoke of bondage.

Behold, I Paul say to you, that if ye be circumcised, Christ shall profit you nothing.

For I testify again to every man that is circumcised, that he is a debtor to do the whole law.

Christ is become of no effect unto you, whosoever of you are justified by the law; you are fallen from grace.

For we through the Spirit wait for the hope of righteousness by faith.

For in Jesus Christ neither circumcision

43

availeth any thing, nor uncircumcision; but faith which worketh by love.

Ye did run well; who did hinder you that ye should not obey the truth?

This persuasion cometh not of him that calleth you. A little leaven leaveneth the whole lump (Galatians 5:1-9).

Revival comes through the pure, holy, unleavened body of Christ.

Wake up!

Get ready for a new day!

The Spirit of God is waiting for the real Church of Jesus Christ to stand up and be strong.

The Spirit of God is waiting for a Church that says, "The more they persecute us, the more they laugh at us, the more they discriminate against us — the stronger and more prosperous we will become!"

It is time to expose the harlot church that dresses up so nicely, that pleases so many people, yet on the inside is full of pollution and decay.

The harlot church is full of leaven, yet Scripture tells us even a little leaven will ruin the whole lump!

A little leaven will pollute our whole mind, our whole will — the entire man will be destroyed by just a bit of leaven.

Jesus said, "Watch out for it."

We Cannot Be Moved!

In my office I have a one hundred-year-old volume of *Foxe's Book of Martyrs*. That amazing book describes the following true story:

In Holland also, in the year 1527, was martyred and burned a good and virtuous widow, named Wendelmuta. This widow, receiving to her heart the brightness of God's grace, by the appearing of the gospel, was apprehended and committed to the Castle of Werden, and shortly after was brought to appear at the general sessions of that country. Several monks were appointed to talk with her, that they might convince her and win her to recant; but she, constantly persisting in the truth, would not be moved.

Many also of her kindred tried to reason with her; among whom there was a noble matron, who loved and favoured dearly the widow in prison. This matron coming, and communing with her, said, "My Wendelmuta, why doest thou not keep silence, and think secretly in thine heart these things which thou believest, that thou mayest prolong here thy days in life?"[3]

What a tempting idea! Just think secretly those things you know will offend the heathen, and then everything will be all right.

Isn't that what we do today?

We sit mutely in our pews while some so-called "Christian" organizations condone sexual intercourse before marriage, homosexual and lesbian preachers, and actually encourage our government to keep the laws on the books that perpetuate the American holocaust on our unborn children.

"Just think it secretly in thy heart that thou might prolong thy days in life."

How did this precious lady answer?

She answered, "Ah, you know not what you say. It is written, 'With the heart man believeth unto righteousness; and with the mouth confession is made unto salvation" (Romans 10:10). And thus, remaining firm and steadfast in her belief and confession, on the twentieth day of November she was condemned by sentence as an heretic, to be burned to ashes, and her goods to be confiscated; she was taking the sentence of her condemnation mildly and quietly.

After she came to the place where she was to be executed, a monk had brought out a cross, desiring her to kiss and worship her God. "I worship," said she, "no wooden god, but only that God which is in heaven;" and so with a joyful countenance, she went to the stake. Then taking the powder, and laying it to her breast, she gave her neck willingly to be bound, and with an ardent prayer commended herself to the hands of God. When the time came that she should be strangled, she modestly closed her eyes, and bowed down her head as one that would take a sleep. The fire then was put to the wood, and she, being strangled, was burned afterwards to ashes, — instead of this life to get the immortal crown in heaven.[4]

Who put Wendelmuta to death?

It was not some screaming band of murderous, cunning politicians.

It was not a gang riot in the inner city.

It was the harlot church!

It was the diluted, ravaged body of a weakened Church, so infested with leaven that it was no longer the Church at all, but a shell of empty and meaningless religiosity!

I do not call lighting candles, or shouting, or marching in and marching out, or standing up and sitting down the body of Christ.

If that is all we have, then it is time to throw our Bibles into a huge pile, set them on fire, have a huge weenie roast and quit!

If this is all the Church is — an infected body of religiosity — then I do not want any part of it.

Leaven is lurking in the darkness like a tempting prostitute, and the harlot church is courting it.

The cry of the '80s was "don't make waves."

I would rather cry with Leonard Ravenhill,

How can you take it easy?

How can you take it easy with a thousand tribes to tell?

How can you take it easy in a world that is bound for hell?

How can you take it easy with the church asleep in its ease?

How can you take it easy?

47

Would someone tell me, please?[5]

It is time we said, "If God be God, then let Him show Himself as God."

And when He shows Himself as God and we are convinced of His Lordship, then let us abandon ourselves to Him.

Let us abandon our hope in material possessions.

Let us abandon our own personal plans and agendas.

Let us die the death of the cross.

Let us resurrect in Him and live this life as if this life really meant nothing ... and eternity really meant something.

Let us count all things but dung for the excellency of Christ, that we might win him!

> *Yea doubtless, and I count all things but loss for the excellency of the knowledge of Christ Jesus my Lord: for whom I have suffered the loss of all things, and do count them but dung, that I may win Christ,*
>
> *And be found in him, not having mine own righteousness, which is of the law, but that which is through the faith of Christ, the righteousness which is of God by faith (Philippians 3:8,9).*

May we expose the diabolical leaven of Satan himself, cleanse it from the Gospel bridge, and lay down planks that are sturdy enough to get humanity out of its weakened existence and into the powerful presence of God.

All leaven has to go.

The great whore of religious traditionalism has to go.

All truth is given by God.

When the Church gets right, we will see the consummation of all truth come into full manifestation. We will see all of Isaiah's power and prophetic insight, all of Jeremiah's fury, all of Hosea's love, all of Daniel's victory, all of Peter's power, all of Paul's revelations.

The very power which was manifested in Christ will all be brought together, and released on this planet in one mighty deluge of revival.

It is the Church's birthright!

But the Church must reach out and take it.

Stop the Devil Cold

The devil has stolen some powerful truths, and it is our responsibility to restore those truths and begin once again to proclaim them. They are the foundational realities, the cornerstones on which God Himself is building a Church against which the gates of hell cannot prevail.

*I will build my church; and the gates of
hell shall not prevail against it (Matthew 16:18).*

The devil cannot stop us when we are born again by the Spirit of God.

The devil cannot stop us when we are filled with the very same Spirit that raised up Christ from the dead *(Romans 8:11).*

49

It is time to cast down phony traditions and religiosity and walk in the reality of the same Spirit that invaded the borrowed tomb of Joseph of Arimathaea, raised up the lifeless body of the Prince of God, and broke the chains of hell and death!

We are the John the Baptists of our generation. No other generation since John the Baptist has had the opportunity to walk this planet and announce that the Kingdom of God is at hand, and there is nothing anyone can do to stop it.

Let the heretics rage on.

Let false prophets prophesy.

The Bible says that in the last days false prophets shall arise and they will say "Here is Christ, and there is Christ" *(Matthew 25:23).*

Let them declare their false truths. We will not be deceived if we are led by the Spirit, filled and walking in the light!

It is time for us to scale the mountainous heights of God for ourselves, to get in the mountain with God where there is quaking, and where the presence of God is overwhelming, and let God reveal Himself to us. God will give us an ear to hear the true prophets, and we will no longer question or wonder what the truth is.

Get in the holy Word and pray for a spirit of wisdom and revelation *(Ephesians 1:17).*

Let the religious dead continue their empty and meaningless ceremonies.

They cannot stop revival once the Church gets right.

They cannot stop the outpouring of the Holy Ghost.

They cannot stop the signs and wonders that will follow those who minister in the name of Jesus.

Verily, verily, I say unto you, He that believeth on me, the works that I do shall he do also; and greater works than these shall he do; because I go unto my Father (John 14:12).

Nothing can stop it.

As surely as the sun came up this morning, the greatest revival we have ever seen, or heard of, or read about is being birthed. God help us to awake and assume our positions as witnesses of the Gospel of Jesus Christ.

I am tired of hearing about what used to be.

It is our turn for revival, and there will never be a day like the one that is dawning.

It is time to repair and restore the broken vessels in the body of Christ.

It is time to get the leaven out!

This is our hour.

This is our day.

The curtain on the scene of life is not going down — it is coming up. This is the finale! This is the last act, and you and I have been chosen by God to be His participants in the final drama of the ages.

There are going to be no greater days than these that are dawning in this endtime generation!

This is it. Stop looking for something else.

51

It is time to get busy. If we are to play the role God has for us in the fulfillment of prophecy we must be ready and willing vessels of honor.

God wants us to change.

To mature.

He wants His Word to come forth from us under a prophetic anointing and unction — to change the world.

But for this move of God to take place, we must get the leaven out of our hearts and out of our lives!

CHAPTER TWO

THE LEAVEN OF THE PHARISEES

But all their works they do
for to be seen of men....
(Matthew 23:5)

Jack stood quietly at the bus stop, waiting for his ride, when two friendly fellows in suits approached him.

"Howdy," one suit said to Jack. "How are you this fine morning?"

"Barely awake," came Jack's reply.

It was just approaching 7:00 a.m., and Jack never seemed to get going until his first cup of coffee at the downtown headquarters.

"I'm Frank Fairasey, and this here's Hank Hipocrite. We are from God's Truth Church in South San Frandango," the suits continued, "and we just wanted you to know that Jesus loves you," they said, extending to Jack a little booklet entitled, *What Must I Do To Be Saved?*

"I appreciate the ministry booklet," Jack replied, "but you might want to give it to someone else. You see, I'm already a born-again Christian. Praise God, I've been serving the Lord for fourteen years now."

"Well, great," the two men replied, shaking Jack's hand vigorously, as if they had just found a long-lost friend.

"Where do you worship?" they asked.

"Down at the Full Gospel Church on 45th Street," Jack replied, starting to wake up, excited at the prospect of talking with these fellow Christians. "Our pastor is John Hoffman."

"Oh," the men replied, visibly stepping back from

Jack as if he had just declared he worshiped at "The Church of Satanic Pleasure, Lust and Child Abuse."

"Then you believe in speaking in tongues?" Frank Fairasey asked very seriously, his smile now totally gone.

"Yes, I do," Jack replied, failing to fully grasp the significance of the question, or the extent of the following reaction.

Without another word, the two men suddenly turned away and started walking down the street, shaking their heads, adjusting their fancy ties, and mumbling to themselves.

A few minutes later, the bus came.

Confused and dejected, Jack climbed on board, feeling a bit dirty, as if he had somehow committed a terrible crime.

As he settled in his seat for the thirty-minute ride to his office headquarters, he wondered how the Church had arrived at such a sorry state.

"What has happened over the years," he wondered, "to bring us to the point where fellow believers cannot even fellowship in love and respect when they discover differences such as speaking in tongues?"

For the rest of his ride, Frank was not able to come up with a satisfactory answer.

"This silly incident will probably bug me all day," he thought to himself as he entered the World Evangelism headquarters where he served as the teaching minister for inner city outreaches in Third World nations.

THE LEAVEN OF THE PHARISEES

The leaven of the Pharisees is all that is phony in religion — the external, outward signs of religiosity — instead of deep commitment from the heart.

The Pharisees performed all the rituals required by law.

They fasted twice each week.

They tithed faithfully.

They prided themselves on their righteousness — but they were only self-righteous. They looked down on the common people, trying to impress the world with their outward show.

The Pharisees even expanded the fringed borders of their prayer shawls. This outward show would be the same today as someone carrying around a big family Bible or some other pretentious show of religiosity.

But all their works they do for to be seen of men: they make broad their phylacteries [prayer boxes], and enlarge the borders of their garments,

And love the uppermost rooms at feasts, and the chief seats in the synagogues,

And greetings in the markets, and to be called of men, Rabbi, Rabbi (Matthew 23:5-7).

The Pharisees loved money.

And the Pharisees also, who were covetous (Luke 16:14).

They sought prominence and flattering titles.

The Pharisees were so biased in their application of the Law that they made it burdensome for the people, insisting that it be observed according to their concepts and traditions.

For they bind heavy burdens and grievous to be borne, and lay them on men's shoulders; but they themselves will not move them with one of their fingers (Matthew 23:4).

The Pharisees completely lost sight of the important matters of the heart such as justice, mercy, faithfulness and the love of God.

Woe unto you, scribes and Pharisees, hypocrites! for ye pay tithe of mint and anise and cummin, and have omitted the weightier matters of the law, judgment, mercy, and faith: these ought ye to have done, and not to leave the other undone (Matthew 23:23).

Jesus clashed with the Pharisees on the observance of the Sabbath *(Matthew 12:1,2)*, on the adherence to tradition *(Matthew 15:1,2)*, and on His association with sinners, tax collectors and other unsavory characters.

But their scribes and Pharisees murmured against his disciples, saying, Why do ye eat and drink with publicans and sinners? (Luke 5:30).

The Pharisees thought that defilement resulted from personal association with persons who did not observe the Law according to their view.

They even found fault with Jesus and His disciples

because they did not practice the traditional ceremony of hand washing.

> For the Pharisees, and all the Jews, except they wash their hands oft, eat not, holding the tradition of the elders.
>
> And when they come from the market, except they wash, they eat not. And many other things there be, which they have received to hold, as the washing of cups, and pots, brasen vessels, and of tables.
>
> Then the Pharisees and scribes asked him, Why walk not thy disciples according to the tradition of the elders, but eat bread with unwashed hands?
>
> He answered, and said unto them, Well hath Esaias prophesied of you hypocrites, as it is written, This people honoureth me with their lips, but their heart is far from me.
>
> Howbeit in vain do they worship me, teaching for doctrines the commandments of men.
>
> For laying aside the commandment of God, ye hold the tradition of men, as the washing of pots and cups: and many other such like things ye do.
>
> And he said unto them, Full well ye reject the commandment of God, that ye may keep your own tradition (Mark 7:3-9).

Jesus frequently exposed the wrong reasoning of the Pharisees, and showed them to be violators of God's law through adherence to their man-made traditions.

Rather than glorifying God for the miraculous cures performed by Christ Jesus on the Sabbath, the Pharisees were filled with rage over what they deemed a violation of the Sabbath Law and, therefore, plotted to kill Him.

To a blind man whom Jesus had cured on the Sabbath, they said, concerning Him,

This man is not of God, because he keepeth not the sabbath day. Others said, How can a man that is a sinner do such miracles? And there was a division among them (John 9:16).

The Pharisees were legalistic and proper to the letter of the law on the outside, but on the inside, their hearts were not righteous, holy or clean.

For I say unto you, That except your righteousness shall exceed the righteousness of the scribes and Pharisees, ye shall in no case enter into the kingdom of heaven (Matthew 5:20).

The Pharisees desperately needed repentance!

They were so spiritually blind, they could not recognize the Son of God. They falsely accused Jesus of casting out demons through the power of the ruler of demons.

But the Pharisees said, He casteth out devils through the prince of the devils (Matthew 9:34).

The Pharisees Still Live!

Modern-day Pharisees are full of dead men's bones: long prayers, long robes, long faces, long tongues, and long ceremonies.

This shallow religiosity is still hampering the ability of the Church today to bring the Gospel to the lost and is damning multiplied millions to hell.

Pharisees are always going to church, but theirs is an external religion of ritual and ceremony that bypasses the true Gospel.

There is only one way to God, and that is through the Gospel of Jesus Christ!

Showing up at church is not enough, and rote prayers will not move heaven.

Leonard Ravenhill said, "We have faulty conversions because we preach a faulty Gospel."

Bypass the Subject of Sin

We have beautifully-ornamented churches with multi-colored, stained-glass windows and golden candelabras on marble altars.

Yet, many do not dance before the Lord anymore.

Let them praise his name in the dance: let them sing praises unto him with the timbrel and harp (Psalm 149:3).

If they shout at all, it is in the back room.

The power of Pentecost has been diluted through the

leaven of the Pharisees. Our crystal chandeliers; plush, padded pews; and new, super-powered, seminary-trained preachers who are schooled to "not make waves" are smothering the fires of revival and hindering the full impact of what God has for us.

There is another way.

It does not matter if we have a Pentecostal name above our door, or a Methodist name, or a Baptist name, or a Catholic name, or a Presbyterian name. It is not what we wear on the outside that matters, but what burns in the sanctuary of our hearts.

Do we have any fire in our hearts?

Do we have any anointing in our hearts?

Do we have any victory, any power in our hearts?

When we do, we will begin to see cripples leaping out of wheelchairs.

We will see blind eyes popping open.

We will see abortion clinics close down because they are unwelcome in our cities.

Pornographers will leave town because they have no business.

I am not talking about showing up at church in the latest suit and tie, I am talking about being born again of the Spirit of God!

Out with the leaven!

We have decisions without conversions.

Decision is reflected in our actions: coming to the altar, raising our hands, repeating the preacher's words

(Pharisees are very good at all of these).

Conversion comes from the heart.

When I ran to the altar at eight years of age, my thirst was quenched with living water, and ever since that time I have been coming back to the well. When God touched my heart, no one had to drag me to church the following week. There was no follow-up visit, and no one had to promise me a chicken dinner to come back.

I was saved to the bone!

How did I get there?

Through the power and conviction of the Holy Spirit, I realized that I was a a dirty, rotten, stinking hunk of sinful flesh doomed to an eternity of hearing the howls and cackles from the bowels of an eternal hell. I heard the preacher tell me that hell is so hot that the fire is never quenched and the worm dieth not; that hell is a place where men gnaw their tongues for pain; and the light is extinguished; and darkness, so black it makes your eyes ache, creeps into your soul.

> *And if thy hand offend thee, cut it off: it is better for thee to enter into life maimed, than having two hands to go into hell, into the fire that never shall be quenched: Where their worm dieth not, and the fire is not quenched (Mark 9:43,44).*

When I give an altar call, I don't say, "Run on down here and God will bless your business. Run on down here and all the financial problems you have will disappear.

Give your heart to God and you will experience God's abundant blessing through a bigger house, a better job, obedient children and a wife who will love you beyond your wildest dreams."

These are the things the Pharisees tell you.

The Bible tells us God cannot bless what is already cursed.

The blessing of God does not come from signing the church roster, shaking the preacher's hand, smiling with the deacons, and dancing little religious dances.

Kneel at the foot of the cross of Christ and plead for His crimson red blood to wash your sins away and for your name to be recorded in the Lamb's Book of Life!

And they shall bring the glory and honour of the nations into it. And there shall in no wise enter into it any thing that defileth, neither whatsoever worketh abomination, or maketh a lie: but they which are written in the Lamb's book of life (Revelation 21:26,27).

It is time to expose the leaven of the Pharisees in the Church.

It is time for preachers to start telling sinners there is still a King who redeems, a cross that bleeds, a hell to shun and a heaven to gain ... that there is still a Holy Spirit who fills and a Lord who is coming again.

Church, don't sit in the doldrums of religious mish-mash one more second. We are playing with a rattlesnake, the very spirit of the whore, and the Bible says that even

64

the Antichrist is finally sickened by her.

Get out of the midst of her, and into the presence of God.

There is a revival on!

Get in the river!

Get in the flow!

Get in the power!

A man needs more than religion, more than seminary training, more than church on Sunday morning, more than fancy church-growth seminars with high-powered, high-paid consultants.

We cannot receive from God through external religiosity. The leaven of the Pharisees has crept into the Church, and no one wants to raise their hands in adoration or bow their knees humbly to the King.

I will tell you why.

We Have Forgotten Our Roots

We do not remember we were sinners.

But God commendeth his love toward us, in that, while we were yet sinners, Christ died for us.

Much more then, being now justified by his blood, we shall be saved from wrath through him (Romans 5:8,9).

We will have an easy time rejoicing again when we remember who we were and who we are today. We will leap to our feet, clapping our hands and shouting, praising

His name with all our might ... when we remember we were on our way to hell, and now we are on our way to heaven through the blood of Jesus Christ.

The Spirit of the Lord is upon me, because he hath anointed me to preach the Gospel to the poor; he hath sent me to heal the broken hearted, to preach deliverance to the captives, and the recovering of sight to the blind, to set at liberty them that are bruised (Luke 4:18).

The Spirit of the Lord is upon us, not the leaven of the Pharisees!

Jesus did not come into this world and die on that tree so we could tell Mr. Big Bucks, "You're just fine. Come on down here and shake my hand," and then hope he puts in a good offering.

Christ died for all of us, including Mr. Big Bucks, who lovingly needs to be told to put down his vodka, and to quit flirting with that secretary at the office.

Preachers, we cannot let fear that Mr. Big Bucks might not come back stop us from letting him hear the truth of the Gospel!

Christ died so that ALL of us would have the opportunity to receive Him and be saved!

Salvation comes when the Holy Spirit of Almighty God rests upon us and draws us to the Father. In too many churches today, there is not enough conviction to get a gnat saved.

Someone asked me recently, "How do I get people

saved in my church?"

The answer was easy: "Tell them the truth. Tell them they are sinners!"

> *For all have sinned, and come short of the glory of God; Being justified freely by his grace through the redemption that is in Christ Jesus: Whom God hath set forth to be a propitiation through faith in his blood, to declare his righteousness for the remission of sins that are past, through the forbearance of God (Romans 3:23-25).*

A preacher came up to me not long ago and said, "Now, Brother Rod, don't you understand? You don't have to scream into the TV camera that those people are sinners. They already know they are sinners."

No, they do not!

I knew I was a sinner because I had godly parents who prayed for me. They took me to the house of God and taught me about Shadrach, Meschach and Abednego; about Daniel and the fiery furnace; about David and his slingshot.

Today, we have a generation raised with daddy on the bar stool and mommy in therapy; with shaved heads on the women and ponytails hanging down the backs of the men; with parents who could scare the demon hordes of hell half to death!

This generation has no sin consciousness.

We party in the bars all weekend, then go to church

on Sunday.

We are a generation that thinks it is normal to sleep around ... abort babies ... rub crystals ... drink alcohol and take drugs ... think God is dead ... and live in homosexual relationships.

It is time to purge ourselves of the leaven of the Pharisees and declare that ... SIN IS SIN.

Shun it!

Run from it!

Jump out of its clutches!

Plead the blood of Jesus and get away from sin or it will destroy you and take you on a path that leads straight to hell.

Preachers, the blood of untold thousands will be required at your hands unless you preach the truth.

When I say unto the wicked, Thou shalt surely die; and thou givest him not warning, nor speakest to warn the wicked from his wicked way, to save his life; the same wicked man shall die in his iniquity; but his blood will I require at thine hand (Ezekiel 3:18).

The Pain of Conviction

"Now, Brother Rod, don't go giving us that condemnation. We are under the blood."

Under the blood? We have scorned and shunned the very convicting power of the Holy Ghost until we are dying as a result of it!

Dying!

Our teenagers are sleeping together on Friday night and running down to the altar on Sunday morning, singing "I am the seed of Abraham."

Why?

Because they are not experiencing the convicting power of God in their church to draw them to anything different.

It is time we had compassion for this sin-sick world, instead of wondering how close we can snuggle up to it.

The body of Christ is acting too much like little Johnny who one night fell out of bed in his sleep. When his mother asked him what happened to make him fall out of bed, his reply was, "I guess I stayed too close to where I got in."

Quit trying to see how close you can live to the world and still be saved.

He that committeth sin is of the devil
(1 John 3:8).

How can we snuggle up to the devil?

It is time to get the leaven of the Pharisees out of our lives.

For the devil sinneth from the beginning.
For this purpose the Son of God was manifested,
that he might destroy the works of the devil
(1 John 3:8).

Have compassion for the country and western singers; pray God convicts them to sing more and more Gospel songs instead of songs about drinking and wild women.

Have compassion for the rock stars. Pray the conviction of God will lead them to salvation and make them mighty witnesses for Christ.

Conviction is a good thing — it reminds us we are sinners, and turns us from the sin.

> *He that is without sin among you, let him first cast a stone at her. And again he stooped down, and wrote on the ground. And they which heard it, being convicted by their own conscience, went out one by one (John 8:7-9).*

The conviction of God is to our spirit what pain is to our body.

Pain is not our enemy; it is only the indication that an enemy exists, and that the enemy is invading our territory. Without pain, we could walk down a sandy beach, cut our foot on a jagged bottle and bleed to death.

This is what is happening in the Church.

We do not feel the pain of conviction, so the leaven of the Pharisees invades our soulish man. We keep walking on in blissful ignorance — while the life-saving blood of Jesus Christ is draining from us.

We cannot pamper sin.

> *Jesus answered them, Verily, verily, I say unto you, Whosoever committeth sin is the servant of sin. And the servant abideth not in the house for ever: but the Son abideth ever (John 8:34,35).*

When we stand before the judgment seat, people will be screaming out the names of their preachers, saying, "Why didn't you tell us those things we were doing would damn our souls? We would have stopped! We would have run from them! You told us they were all right. Why didn't you tell us?"

Root out the whore of religious traditionalism before it damns untold millions to hell.

Jesus said, "Beware of the leaven of Pharisees" — the external traditions of religion, the seemingly healthy bodies composed of dead men's bones.

Beware of ceremonies without meaning.

Beware of long prayers uttered only so those around us can hear them and be impressed with our vocabulary and our knowledge of Scripture.

The Word says to beware those who *for a pretence make long prayers (Mark 12:40).*

Beware of the silk-suited glitter of the false prophets on television who will pray for us only as long as we continue to send them our money.

Beware of the leaven of the Pharisees.

Beware of volumes of preaching followed by voids of action.

Beware of great swelling words devoid of anointing or power.

Beware of false images of God.

We cannot believe anything about God we want to believe. To believe anything other than what the Bible says is to worship a false image. The Israelites made up their minds who they thought God was, and then bowed before a golden calf!

Beware of wolves in sheep's clothing ... clouds with no water ... false prophets.

Discern the Move of God

"Oh, but Brother Rod, this prophet told me my name."

Some Christians are so gullible.

False prophets come from everywhere, renting out auditoriums, displaying signs that read: "John Doe, Prophet of God."

And some vulnerable Christians — who are too lazy to read the Bible, who are too lazy to enter the prayer closet, who are too lazy to have a relationship with God, and who are satisfied with external religion — go to these meetings to get a word from God.

They come back home, so excited and thrilled that someone told them their name.

I ask them, "Didn't you know your name before you went to the meeting?"

"Yes, but he told me my address. He told me where I lived," they reply with deep conviction.

One Sunday morning I walked out into our congregation, approached a lady I had never seen before, and told her her name.

"Have I ever met you before?" I asked.

"No," she replied, her voice trembling with excitement.

"Then how did I know your name?" I questioned. Before she could answer, I said, "By the way, you live at this address and your phone number is thus-and-so."

She almost fell out in the aisle!

The ushers had to help her.

When the commotion died down, I again started to speak with this lady, whom I will call Mary.

"Now, Mary, have I ever met you before?"

"No, Pastor, you have not," she replied, gasping for breath she was so excited.

"Then how did I know your name, your address and your phone number?" I asked her.

"God must have told you," she replied innocently.

"Is that right?" I said. "Mary, look over your shoulder there. What do you see?"

"Well, I see a television camera," she replied with a little hesitation.

"Mary, would you take out your checkbook like you did during the offering?" I asked. Mary then took out her checkbook and opened it up. I continued, "Now Mary, when you were writing out your check, that television camera became my eyes and zoomed in on your name, address and phone number. When that usher walked up here, he handed me a piece of paper on which the television operator wrote where you were, what your

73

name was, and what your address was. The TV camera caught that information, and the usher brought it to me."

By this time, Mary was a bit embarrassed, but certainly much wiser.

I would never do this to try to embarrass or confuse anyone, but it is critical that we learn to use wisdom so we are not so easily deceived by false prophets.

Do not be deceived!

The camera man is not God.

For every true prophet, there will be a false one. The only hope for the Church to discern the difference is to know God.

How?

Get alone until you are not alone anymore.

Pray in the Holy Ghost.

Fast and pray and study God's Word, and the Holy Spirit will lead you into all truth ... then you will know the Spirit of truth from the spirit of error.

> *But strong meat belongeth to them that are*
> *of full age, even those who by reason of use*
> *have their senses exercised to discern both*
> *good and evil (Hebrews 5:14).*

Be strong! Sharp! Accurate!

We are the people of God ... the final generation!

Learn to hear God's voice, and declare His Word to a dying generation.

Church, beware of the leaven of the Pharisees.

Inside, they are full of death.

Evangelism Without Revival

The Church frequently calls its evangelistic meetings "revivals," yet they have no power or words to revive. True revival rehabilitates, reconstructs, rejuvenates, refreshes, restores, resurrects, renews and repairs!

Paul said,

And my speech and my preaching was not with enticing words of man's wisdom, but in demonstration of the Spirit and of power (1 Corinthians 2:4).

Paul knew the Gospel was more than preaching; it was a demonstration of God's power!

The great Lutheran church did not begin because it had a fancy tent, a good-sounding band and brightly colored lights to attract a crowd.

It began in the Spirit.

The Pentecostal revival that shook this nation in the early 1900s began in the Spirit.

Revival begins in the Spirit — not with fancy tricks, air-conditioned churches, empty words, dead ceremonies and irrelevant rituals.

Stop looking for an exciting new preacher, or a new denomination.

We began in the Spirit ... we will finish in the Spirit!

Resist the leaven.

Tear it out!

Root it out!

Let the fruit of the Holy Spirit grow in your heart.

We can become the coals of revival — flaming embers full of the power of God.

But we must first rebuke the leaven of the Pharisees — false pride, attitudes of separation and superiority, clinging to meaningless traditions and superficial rituals that do not bring forth fruit.

Out with the leaven and in with the greatest revival this world has ever seen — through the power of the Holy Ghost — to reach the lost in a dying world!

Receive the power of the Holy Ghost!

Receive an impartation of faith, and be changed!

No longer does the Church have to be deceived by Pharisees and false prophets.

Dedication Without Separation

Come out and be ye separate (Hebrews 7:26).

And be not conformed to this world: but be ye transformed by the renewing of your mind, that ye may prove what is that good, and acceptable, and perfect, will of God (Romans 12:2).

The only way to fully understand the will of God for our lives is by the renewing of the mind by the miraculous transformation that comes as a result of separation from the world and union with Him. The Bible tells us God's will, but a mind that has not been renewed cannot understand it.

Spiritual death is separation from the life flow of God. There are some people who are born-again that are walking, breathing, talking dead men.

For to be carnally minded is death; but to be spiritually minded is life and peace. Because the carnal mind is enmity against God: for it is not subject to the law of God, neither indeed can be. So then they that are in the flesh cannot please God (Romans 8:6-8).

Our soul is composed of the mind, the will and the emotions. When we are born again, our mind is not born again, our will is not born again, our emotions are not born again. It is only our spirit man that is born again.

That is why Paul said,

I beseech you therefore, brethren, by the mercies of God, that ye present your bodies a living sacrifice, holy, acceptable unto God, which is your reasonable service (Romans 12:1).

To be carnally minded does not mean we spiritually cease to exist. It means we are separated from the life flow of God. A carnal mind robs us of our joy, our peace, our relationship with the Father, our righteousness.

It is time for the Church to stop acting like a Ping-Pong ball on the table of life, allowing a carnal mind to whack us from one side to the other.

It is time to stand up for righteousness and take control of our carnal nature and be delivered from the bondage of the fear of death. The power of carnality has been broken by the cross of Christ.

From Genesis to Revelation, Jesus said, "The words I say are spirit. They are life."

His Words will drive death and the grave out of the body, the mind, and the spirit.

His Words are alive.

In him was life; and the life was the light of men. And the light shineth in darkness; and the darkness comprehended it not (John 1:4,5).

It is not so important what is done for God, but what is done by God. It is not the programs, propaganda, pep rallies or perky personnel that count, but rather, God's power!

Preparation Without Expectation

Henceforth there is laid up for me a crown of righteousness, which the Lord, the righteous judge, shall give me at that day: and not to me only, but unto all them also that love his appearing (2 Timothy 4:8).

We are to love His appearing.

We should not be so concerned with bringing in the Kingdom as in bringing back the King.

Waiting at the airport to pick up a stranger or business associate is one thing; but if a loved one is on board the aircraft, we have a different view, a different excitement!

View the end of the age with that same excitement.

The King is coming.

Welcome the King!

Fast and Pray

Fast, pray and study God's Word to grow in maturity and to be able to discern the Spirit of truth.

Kneel at the foot of the cross of Christ and plead for His crimson blood to wash your sins away.

We need a spiritual revolution against the leaven of the Pharisees to free ourselves once and for all from the spirit of the world, and to enter into the Spirit of the Lord.

The Spirit of the Lord is upon me, because he hath anointed me to preach the gospel to the poor; he hath sent me to heal the brokenhearted, to preach deliverance to the captives, and recovering of sight to the blind, to set at liberty them that are bruised (Luke 4:18).

We are all called to bring the Gospel to the poor; to bring deliverance to those addicted to drugs and alcohol; to remove the blinders from the eyes of the atheists, the abortion advocates, and the homosexuals; and to minister to all that are hurting and abused.

It will not happen until we get the leaven of the Pharisees out of the Church, and out of our own lives.

Fasting is not just a physical fast from food.

Is not this the fast that I have chosen? to loose the bands of wickedness, to undo the

heavy burdens, and to let the oppressed go free,
and that ye break every yoke? (Isaiah 58:6).

We do not understand fasting in the body of Christ. Most people think it is a hunger strike against God — they are going to starve until God does something. That is a real good way to die, because God is not impressed by how little we eat. It makes little difference to God whether we have one or two deluxe hamburgers.

Fasting is the denial of the natural man that brings our body and soul into submission to our spirit man. This allows us to hear what God has been trying to say to us all along, and to be conformed to the will and the image of His dear Son.

We do not fast from food, or television, or golf, or Sunday afternoon football to change God's mind.

We cannot change the mind of God by fasting.

We move God by faith — the steadfast confidence, trust and assurance in the fact that God said what He meant and meant what He said, and that He will back up His Word.

Fasting is the denial of the natural man. Fasting is the process of purification that disciplines our carnal nature.

Why do we fast?

To loose the bands of wickedness ... to undo the heavy burdens ... to let the oppressed go free ... to break every yoke.

Once the natural man has been brought into

submission to the spirit man, we can begin to walk in the reality of the next verse.

Is it not to deal thy bread to the hungry, and that thou bring the poor that are cast out to thy house? when thou seest the naked, that thou cover him; and that thou hide not thyself from thine own flesh? (v.7).

To deal thy bread to the hungry means we are willing to sacrifice what we have to help those in need.

It means we are willing to stop walking around in our beautiful, clean robes pretending everything is beautiful and instead put on our jeans and hard hats and take a walk in the mud of life.

When the Church starts functioning according to verse seven, then we can claim the promises of God in verses eight and nine.

Then shall thy light break forth as the morning, and thine health shall spring forth speedily: and thy righteousness shall go before thee; the glory of the Lord shall be thy reward. Then shalt thou call, and the Lord shall answer; thou shalt cry, and he shall say, Here I am (vv. 8,9).

A study of this passage shows that in less time than it takes our minds to send that impulse to our tongues to speak His Name — in between our minds and our tongues — He has already answered!

Why are we in healing lines all the time?

81

Because we are not living the truths of Isaiah 58!
Some of us are sick every third day.

God is looking for those who will obey His Word. He says, "If you do not deal your bread to the hungry; if you do not clothe the naked; if you do not take care of the disadvantaged; if you do not turn your face from the naked and cover them; if you do not minister to those in need — then you will walk in darkness and your health will not spring forth."

That is what the Bible says!

They are not my words; they are God's. Only through obedience to God's Word will we receive the blessings He has promised.

Some people are not healed because they do not care about anyone else but themselves.

Others are never sick because they are dealing their bread every day: missions, inner city outreaches, food pantrys, clothing pantrys, blankets and hot food for shelters.

The leaven of the Pharisees shuns the sick, avoids the poor, and walks across the street from the naked.

A certain man went down from Jerusalem to Jericho, and fell among thieves, which stripped him of his raiment, and wounded him, and departed, leaving him half dead.

And by chance there came down a certain priest that way: and when he saw him, he passed by on the other side.

And likewise a Levite, when he was at the

*place, came and looked on him, and passed by
on the other side.*

*But a certain Samaritan, as he journeyed,
came where he was: and when he saw him,
he had compassion on him,*

*And went to him, and bound up his
wounds, pouring in oil and wine, and set him
on his own beast, and brought him to an inn,
and took care of him (Luke 10:30-34).*

In this final hour, God is challenging us to exchange
the leaven of the Pharisees for the love of the good Samaritan.

He is challenging us to sow into the lives of the disadvantaged, to clothe the naked, and to bring food to the hungry.

The Church is not the four walls where we worship.

The Church is a caring body of believers that must reach out to the hurting and the desperate. People who do not have enough food or clothes, people who need the ministering touch of the saints, desperately need a church free of the leaven of the Pharisees that will minister liberally and joyfully to them.

The Pharisees love money.

The blood-bought Church of Jesus Christ gives it away to warm the back of someone who is cold and to put food in the belly of someone who has not eaten for three days.

That is a Gospel the Pharisees could never recognize

or understand!

Now is the hour for the Church to thank God for the opportunity to give of our bread.

Now is the hour for us to joyfully and liberally sow our seed for the spread of the Gospel so that the covenant promise of Isaiah 58 may be fulfilled and people may be fed, not only spiritually, but naturally.

Now is the hour for healing to be manifested in the incredible power of the full light of God.

Now is the hour for the leaven of the Pharisees to be rooted out, once and for all.

CHAPTER THREE

THE LEAVEN OF THE SADDUCEES

*For the Sadducees say that there is
no resurrection, neither angel,
nor spirit....
(Acts 23:8)*

"Mommy, What Are We?"

Little Joseph was at the age that challenges every parent's ability to answer probing questions. This particular day, as he drank his milk and ate his freshly-baked chocolate chip cookies after school, Joey was in another one of his questioning moods.

"Mommy, what are we?" Joseph asked.

"What do you mean, dear?" his mother asked, not sure what Joseph was talking about. "We are human beings, if that's what you mean."

"Oh, I know that," Joey replied. "I mean, what are we? Sam says his family is Christian, and that they believe in Jesus Christ. What are we?"

"Well," his mother replied without any hesitation, "we are not Christians, that's for sure. We are not anything like that."

"How come?" Joey asked.

"Because we don't need that stuff," his mama replied. "We don't need to believe in a heaven or a hell or some god to be nice to people. We just do the best we can."

"Well, if we are not Christians, then where do we go when we die?" Joey replied, taking another sip of his milk. "Sam says he's going to heaven. Mommy, where will we go?"

"We're not going anywhere," the mother answered her son as confidently as she could. "Some people need to believe in a heaven to make them feel good. We don't.

The truth is, Joey, that when you and I die, we will just die. That's all there is to it. We don't go anywhere. We just cease to live, like your hamster did last summer."

"I don't know if I like that much," Joey replied. "Why can't we be Christians so we can go to heaven?"

"Because we don't need it," his mama snapped, obviously irritated. She quickly left the kitchen, shaking her head, as she started vacuuming the living room.

Joey sat at the table and continued his snack.

"If I don't need heaven and God," Joey wondered, "then how come both sound so good?"

Joey walked across the kitchen and put the milk carton back in the refrigerator.

As he went upstairs to his room, he was still thinking about his friend Sam.

"I think Sam's lucky to have God and to go to heaven when he dies," he mused. "Who wants to just disappear like a hamster? Maybe, when I get older, if this heaven thing is still around, and if this God guy will have me, I think I would like to become one of those Christians."

THE LEAVEN OF THE SADDUCEES

The Sadducees were a prominent religious sect of the Jewish priesthood during the time of Jesus Christ.

Then the high priest rose up, and all they that were with him (which is the sect of the Sadducees), and were filled with indignation, and laid their hands on the apostles, and put them in the common prison (Acts 5:17,18).

Like the Pharisees, the Sadducees opposed Jesus and His disciples. However, the Sadducees did not believe in the supernatural, thus rejecting the resurrection from the dead, and denying the existence of angels.

For the Sadducees say that there is no resurrection, neither angel, nor spirit: but the Pharisees confess both (Acts 23:8).

To try to catch Jesus in a theological puzzle concerning the existence of the resurrection, the Sadducees made up a hypothetical example of a woman who married six brothers-in-law after her original husband died. The Sadducees thought this ridiculous scenario would stump Jesus on the theological question of the resurrection, and on heaven itself.

The same day came to him the Sadducees, which say that there is no resurrection, and asked him,

Saying, Master, Moses said, If a man die, having no children, his brother shall marry his wife, and raise up seed unto his brother.

Now there were with us seven brethren: and the first, when he had married a wife, deceased, and, having no issue, left his wife unto his brother:

Likewise the second also, and the third, unto the seventh.

And last of all the woman died also.

Therefore in the resurrection whose wife shall she be of the seven? for they all had her (Matthew 22:23-28).

Jesus recognized the Sadducees were attempting to mock and trick Him, so He immediately silenced them by referring to the Scriptures the Sadducees professed to study and accept.

But Jesus replied to them, You are wrong, because you know neither the Scriptures nor God's power. For in the resurrected state neither do [men] nor are [women] given in marriage, but they are as the angels in heaven (Matthew 22:29,30 AMP).

Jesus did not stop with the explanation that there would not be marriages in heaven. Knowing the hypocritical nature of the Sadducees, He also refuted their contention concerning the resurrection from the dead.

But as touching the resurrection of the dead, have ye not read that which was spoken unto you by God, saying, I am the God of

*Abraham, and the God of Isaac, and the God
of Jacob? God is not the God of the dead, but
of the living (Matthew 22:31,32).*

Because the Sadducees, contrary to the Word of
God, vehemently denied the supernatural, especially the
resurrection of the dead, it is little wonder they were "so
sad, you see!"

Did Not Keep the Law

The Sadducees needed to produce constant fruit
befitting repentance because they, like the Pharisees, had
failed to keep God's law.

*But when he saw many of the Pharisees
and Sadducees come to his baptism, he said
unto them, O generation of vipers, who hath
warned you to flee from the wrath to come?
Bring forth therefore fruits meet for repentance
(Matthew 3:7,8).*

A viper is a highly poisonous snake. Jesus compared
the Sadducees to a "generation of vipers" because He
saw them as both dangerous and deadly. Jesus knew you
could not live contrary to Scripture. The Sadducees chose
to ignore the Word of God, refusing to believe in heaven
or hell.

*Lay not up for yourselves treasures upon
earth, where moth and rust doth corrupt, and
where thieves break through and steal: But lay
up for yourselves treasures in heaven, where*

neither moth nor rust doth corrupt, and where thieves do not break through nor steal (Matthew 6:19,20).

Because the Sadducees chose to keep their treasures on earth, and ignore the reality of heaven, they could only experience rust and corruption. Christ Himself compared the polluted preaching of the Sadducees to unwanted leaven.

Then Jesus said unto them, Take heed and beware of the leaven of the Pharisees and of the Sadducees (Matthew 16:6).

And again,

How is it that ye do not understand that I spake it not to you concerning bread, that ye should beware of the leaven of the Pharisees and of the Sadducees? Then understood they how he bade them not beware of the leaven of bread, but of the doctrine of the Pharisees and of the Sadducees (Matthew 16:11,12).

The Sadducees were so opposed to the teachings of Christ that they took the lead in trying to stop the spread of Christianity after the death and resurrection of Jesus.

But that it spread no further among the people, let us straitly threaten them, that they speak henceforth to no man in this name (Acts 4:17).

The god of this world had clearly made the Sadducees blind to the truth.

*But if our gospel be hid, it is hid to them
that are lost: In whom the god of this world
hath blinded the minds of them which believe
not, lest the light of the glorious gospel of
Christ, who is the image of God, should shine
unto them (2 Corinthians 4:3,4).*

The Sadducees were ignorant of Satan's devices and, like Adam and Eve in the Garden of Eden, they fell prey to his lies and deceptions.

*Lest Satan should get an advantage of
us: for we are not ignorant of his devices
(2 Corinthians 2:11).*

Jesus knew the Sadducees were liars, and that they desperately needed to know the truth of the Gospel. That is why he so clearly told them, in so many ways, that there is a price to pay for sin, and that the payment will be extracted for all eternity!

*When I say unto the wicked, O wicked man,
thou shalt surely die; if thou dost not speak to
warn the wicked from his way, that wicked man
shall die in his iniquity; but his blood will I require at thine hand (Ezekiel 33:8).*

The Reality of Heaven

The leaven of the Sadducees has no place in the New Testament Church.

We need to once again become a Church that believes

in the Holy Ghost and a literal heaven and hell ... a Church on fire, with the supernatural demonstration of the gifts of the Spirit, laying hands on the sick and casting out devils!

Ira Stamphill, the great hymn writer of the Church, said it this way: "I've got a mansion just over the hilltop, in that bright land where we will never grow old. And some day yonder we will never more wander, but walk on streets that are purest gold."[1]

We need a Church anxious to go to that heavenly city that rises 1,500 miles high, with walls made of jasper, and gates made of a single pearl 300 feet high. We will stroll down heavenly boulevards of gold, and drink from the river of life. We will lay our weapons down and war no more.

The former things will all pass away, and standing at the gate of that celestial city with the nail prints in His hands, the resurrected King of Kings and Lord of Lords is going to greet us and say, "No, no, no. Do not walk in here with those tears running down your cheeks. Let Me wipe them out of your eyes. In this city there's no more weeping, no more crying, no more sickness, no more pain, no more death. You are going to joyfully leap forever over the everlasting hills of God!"

And he that sat upon the throne said, Behold, I make all things new. And he said unto me, Write: for these words are true and faithful. And he said unto me, It is done. I am Alpha and Omega, the beginning and the end. I

will give unto him that is athirst of the foun-
tain of the water of life freely (Revelation
21:5,6).

The Reality of Hell

There was an old beggar who sat at the gate of a rich man every day. The old man only hoped for some of the crumbs that fell from the sumptuous suppers of that rich man's table. However, the rich man was embarrassed by the presence of the beggar, and never lifted a hand to help him. When the wealthy man's affluent friends came by, they would say to him, "You should do something about that poor beggar out there by your gate. It is embarrassing to see him when I come here."

The Bible says the rich man was in hell when he died, and he lifted up his voice and cried, "I am tormented in these flames, but I see over in Abraham's bosom that old beggar man named Lazarus who laid by my gate every day. Please, please go over there and tell him to dip his finger in a little bit of water and touch even just a drop of it to my tongue. I am so tormented in these flames."

And he cried and said, Father Abraham,
have mercy on me, and send Lazarus, that he
may dip the tip of his finger in water, and cool
my tongue; for I am tormented in this flame. But
Abraham said, Son, remember that thou in thy
lifetime receivedst thy good things, and likewise

Lazarus evil things: but now he is comforted, and thou art tormented (Luke 16:24,25).

There are little animals that live in England called moles. They use their fur to make beautiful garments. Any time you want, you can just walk out in the field and pick them up.

Why? You can pick them up because they can't see to run from you. They are born blind. Their eyes are closed, and they spend their entire lives in abject darkness.

Those little creatures are killed by hitting them in the head with a mallet. When they die, a strange thing happens — for the first time in their existence, their eyes come open.

The Sadducees of this world do not believe in eternity; they do not believe in heaven or hell. They reject the Son of God and His Church, and they criticize His people and say, "I don't believe."

But one of these days, their eyes are going to be opened wide, and they are going to recognize that the Bible is true, infallible and inerrant. They are going to realize that God does not need our finite minds to rearrange it and make it different than what it is.

It is time the Church returned to Bible basics, and believed God said what He meant and meant what He said!

Two key factors in recognizing a cult are the denial of Jesus as God's Son; and the denial of a literal, burning hell. Many of the false religions of this world deny hell, and offer instead the revolving door of reincarnation.

I am not looking for a revolving door.

Once I leave this planet, I am not looking for a way back.

I am looking for the exit door.

The Great Transgression

The Sadducees presumed to know more about the nature of God than God Himself!

They claimed, contrary to Scripture, that man would not face an eternal resurrection.

They claimed, contrary to Scripture, that angels did not exist.

They claimed, contrary to Scripture, that Jesus Christ Himself was a false prophet.

Beware the leaven of the Sadducees; it is as deadly as the poison of a viper!

David once asked God to deliver him from the great transgression.

> *Then shall I be upright, and I shall be innocent from the great transgression (Psalm 19:13).*

What was that great transgression?

David committed adultery, but that was not the great transgression.

> *And David sent messengers, and took her [Bathsheba, who was Uriah the Hittite's wife];*

and she came in unto him, and he lay with her
(2 Samuel 11:4).

David was a murderer; he had Uriah slain. But that was not the great transgression.

And he [David] wrote in the letter, saying,
Set ye Uriah in the forefront of the hottest
battle, and retire ye from him, that he may be
smitten, and die (2 Samuel 11:15).

David committed a cold-blooded, premeditated murder, yet when he cried out, "Lord, deliver me from the great transgression," he was not speaking about murder or adultery.

There is a transgression — a sin — greater than adultery and greater than premeditated, cold-blooded murder.

David's great transgression was that he would presume something to be true about God that was not true.

It is this same great transgression that fuels the phony doctrines of the Sadducees, giving energy to their sin of presumption.

The Church and the secular world are full of the leaven of the Sadducees.

Keep back thy servant also from presump-
tuous sins; let them not have dominion over me
(Psalm 19:13).

We want to build a little golden calf of a god inside our own philosophy ... inside the framework of our own intellectualism. We want to build a little god for ourselves and say, "Well, that is what I think God is. That is how I think God responds. I do not think God would do that. And, I think God really wants us to do this."

With all due respect, it does not make any difference to God what we think or what we believe about Him!

He gave us the Bible with sixty-six books in it, and the Bible declares, "This is Who I am and how I respond. Get in my Book and know me."

We think God winks at our ignorance of spiritual matters, but the Bible says,

> *My people are destroyed for lack of knowl-*
> *edge: because thou hast rejected knowledge,*
> *I will also reject thee, that thou shalt be no*
> *priest to me: seeing thou hast forgotten the law*
> *of thy God, I will also forget thy children*
> *(Hosea 4:6).*

We think God will welcome unsaved Jews into heaven with open arms, but the Bible says,

> *He that believeth on him is not con-*
> *demned: but he that believeth not is con-*
> *demned already, because he hath not believed*
> *in the name of the only begotten Son of God*
> *(John 3:18).*

Married couples think God will overlook their adulterous affairs. Singles think God will overlook their sexual indiscretions. Homosexuals think God will overlook their transgressions.

Yes, God loves the sinner and hates the sin.

But, the Bible also says,

Know ye not that the unrighteous shall not inherit the kingdom of God? Be not deceived: neither fornicators, nor idolaters, nor adulterers, nor effeminate, nor abusers of themselves with mankind, nor thieves, nor covetous, nor drunkards, nor revilers, nor extortioners, shall inherit the kingdom of God (1 Corinthians 6:9,10).

The religious Sadducees of our day want to dress Jesus up in blue jeans and send Him strolling merrily on His way down to the neighborhood shopping mall to buy the latest name-brand tennis shoes and fancy jacket.

But that is not the Jesus I need.

I need a bleeding, dying, resurrecting, life-giving, life-changing, blind-man healing, leper-cleansing Jesus!

I need a Jesus who can leap through time and space into the fiery trials of my life, and catch me before the crackling flames kindle upon my feet.

We are never going to dream up the Jesus I serve in our own thoughts.

David revealed that the greatest idolatry and greatest sin we can ever commit is to presume something about God that is not true.

That is precisely what the leaven of the Sadducees is doing today.

Who is America's God?

Time magazine recently published an article titled, "The Baby Boom Goes Back to Church."[2]

Well, I am glad Americans are going to church, but I must admit I am concerned about who they are going to find when they get there. I am just not very confident that they are looking for or will find the Jesus I serve.

No, I believe they are looking for a comfortable Jesus, a Jesus who is going to put them over the top in their business, who is going to heal their body, who is going to pop up on the primrose path of spiritual experience and materially bless them like they have never been blessed before.

New cars ... new boats ... bigger homes ... bigger bank accounts ... more self-confidence seminars and feel-good videos ... and more church socials and chicken dinners.

That is not the Jesus I am serving.

The Jesus I serve declares,

> *If any man will come after me, let him deny himself, and take up his cross, and follow me (Matthew 16:24).*

That is not the route of the "secret-service Christian," hiding safely in the sanctuary of the church, all the while shouting "Bless me, bless me, bless me."

We cannot make God who we want Him to be.

We cannot conform the image of God to our idea of who He is. He said,

> *For my thoughts are not your thoughts,*

101

*neither are your ways my ways, saith the Lord
(Isaiah 55:8).*

If you want to know who He is, He is defined in His myriad of names.

"I am Jehovah Ropheka; I am the God that healeth thee."

"I am Jehovah Tsidkenu; I am the Lord God, your righteousness."

"I am Jehovah M'kaddesh; I am the Lord God, your holiness."

"I am Jehovah Shammah; I am the God who is always present with you."

"I am Jehovah Shalom; I am the God of your peace."

"I am Jehovah Rohi; I am the Lord God your shepherd."

"I am Jehovah Jireh; I am the God who supplies before there is a need."

He said, "I am the lion of the tribe of Judah. I was conceived in the virgin womb of a young girl named Mary. I was conceived of the very Spirit of the living God. I plunged into time from eternity. I came to earth, and the purpose for my coming is this: I came to save my people from their sins ... that is the reason I am here."

God does not wink at your sin.

He does not understand when you are too busy for His Word, when you are too busy to gather yourself together in the local assembly of believers.

We have had a palatable Jesus preached for so long that we hardly recognize the real One when we are exposed to Him.

How sad, you see.

Get the leaven of the Sadducees out of the Church and get in touch with the real Jesus.

Ten Great Guidelines!

No one wants to talk about the Ten Commandments anymore.

"Well now, Brother Rod, that is the Old Covenant."

The difference between the Old Covenant and the New Covenant is that God gave us the Law in the Old Covenant, but we had no power to keep it.

In the New Covenant, He fulfilled the Law by giving us power to keep it.

Instead of following the Ten Commandments given to us by God when He brought the Jews out of the land of Egypt and the house of bondage, we have rewritten them. We have said, "Thou shalt not, ordinarily," "Thou shalt not, unless" and "Thou shalt not, except."

Like the Sadducees, we have tried to rewrite Scripture!

There is no "sometime"; there is no "unless" in Scripture.

How can we change the Ten Commandments? They were written with the finger of God!

103

And he gave unto Moses, when he had made an end of communing with him upon mount Sinai, two tables of testimony, tables of stone, written with the finger of God (Exodus 31:18).

And the tables were the work of God, and the writing was the writing of God, graven upon the tables (Exodus 32:16).

1.   The Bible plainly says:

I am the Lord thy God, which brought thee out of the land of Egypt, from the house of bondage. Thou shalt have none other gods before me (Deuteronomy (5:6,7).

That means no other god!

Not the god of business, not the god of finance, not the god of achievement, not the god of social life, not the gods of alcohol and drug abuse, not the gods of religion ... not the false god of the Sadducees who condemns some sins and freely overlooks others.

The only God we can have before us is the God of the Old and New Testaments, the God who is the same yesterday, today and forever.

2.   The Bible plainly says:

Thou shalt not make thee any graven image (Deuteronomy 5:8).

We do not worship golden calves. We do not worship the false images of a god we have built and constructed in our philosophical and intellectual minds!

The Sadduces bow down and pay allegiance to these false gods of their own concoction, while Jehovah God sits on His heavenly throne...

...visiting the iniquity of the fathers upon the children unto the third and fourth generation of them that hate me, and shewing mercy unto thousands of them that love me and keep my commandments (Deuteronomy 5:9,10).

3.   The Bible plainly says:

Thou shalt not take the name of the Lord thy God in vain (Deuteronomy 5:11).

We all understand that this commandment means that we are not to utter any profanity — to swear or use vulgar language.

But there is more to it than that.

The Bible says,

And these signs shall follow them that believe; in my name shall they cast out devils; they shall speak with new tongues; They shall take up serpents; and if they drink any deadly thing, it shall not hurt them; they shall lay hands on the sick, and they shall recover (Mark 16:17).

We will cast out devils in His Name.

105

"Well, we do not do that at our church, Brother Rod."

Why not?

The Bible says we are to do it.

To presume God is something different than He says He is, is to heap the sin of idolatry on our heads. If we believe in the Name of Jesus and do not want to take His Name in vain, then we must cast out devils.

When we are in disagreement with the Word of God, we take His Name in vain.

The heinous crimes being committed in our society, the abuse of drugs and alcohol, the production and purchase of pornography, the abortion of babies — are all being sped along their hellish, damnable track by one thing — the presence of demonic power on the face of the earth.

And we have a Church that wants to hide from it!

Jesus said these signs shall follow us when we believe.

We will cast out devils.

We will speak with new tongues.

We will lay hands on the sick.

"Well now, Brother Rod, I just do not believe in laying hands on people. We just don't do it, and I don't believe God expects it."

We dreamed up these lies in our presumptuous, intellectual minds. We did not get them out of the Book. I have my degrees hanging on my wall, but I am trying to forget about them.

Why?

Because God is beyond our minds. He is beyond our finite capability to intellectualize Him. God cannot be intellectualized. He cannot be explained.

He is not to be explained, but to be exalted!

Once when I was traveling I ate some spoiled food. The doctor said, "If you had arrived at the hospital a few minutes later, you would have been dead."

As I was rushed to the hospital, I repeated over and over, "In Jesus' name, in Jesus' name, in Jesus' name." I was praying the name that is above every name. At that name, every knee must bow and every tongue must confess that Jesus Christ is Lord!

I called on the holy name of Jesus in my time of need, and He heard my cry. As Christians, it is time we recognized that using God's name in a profane manner is more than cursing.

We put "Christian" in front of our name, but the greatest profanity is to take His name and fail to work in its power!

Having a form of godliness, but denying the power thereof: from such turn away. For of this sort are they which creep into houses, and lead captive silly women laden with sins, led away with divers lust, ever learning, and never able to come to the knowledge of the truth (2 Timothy 3:5-7).

We file into church, go through all the motions, go through our little religious ceremonies, soothe our consciences, then go out just as depressed, just as sick, just as lonely, just as hopeless as when we came in.

It is time the church became the Church.

Our children have a right to see an outpouring of the demonstration of a living God, a God who is not just an idea floating around out there in a wisp of nothingness, but is a real God.

The problem is not the atheist shaking his fist in the face of God and exclaiming "God does not exist."

The problem is not the agnostic who says, "Well, there is a God out there, but He does not care anything about me."

Far more insidious are the so-called Christians who, despite that outward facade are virtual strangers to the character and nature of the God they claim to know and serve.

They have a form of godliness, but they deny the power thereof.

They, more than anyone else, take the name of our precious Lord in vain.

4. **The Bible plainly says:**

Keep the sabbath day to sanctify it, as the Lord thy God hath commanded thee (Deuteronomy 5:12).

Do not bow down to the shrine of Sunday football games and do thy worship. Thou shalt not remember to wax thy car on the Sabbath day. Thou shalt not use Sunday as the day for shopping or cutting the lawn.

Sunday is God's day — not from 10:00 a.m. until noon — but all day.

5.   The Bible plainly says:

Honour thy father and thy mother, as the Lord thy God hath commanded thee; that thy days may be prolonged, and that it may be well with thee, in the land which the Lord thy God giveth thee (Deuteronomy 5:16).

Stop creating your own Gospel!

God did not say to honor our parents until we hit thirteen, or until we no longer agreed with their rules.

He said to honor them, period.

By fulfilling this commandment, God promises us that "it may be well with thee" in the place where we live.

6.   The Bible plainly says:

Thou shalt not kill (Deuteronomy 5:17).

The orginal Hebrew here clearly states that no murder shall be committed.

This commandment is not talking about times of war when soldiers fight to protect and preserve their nation, or capital punishment as prescribed by law for crimes such as murder, rape or incest.

Suicide is not allowed, according to God's law.

Abortions are not allowed, according to God's law, yet unborn babies are being slaughtered at the rate of three per minute, twenty-four hours a day![3]

The leaven of the Sadducees has permeated and polluted even one of the clearest mandates of God: Thou shalt not kill!

7. The Bible plainly says:

Neither shalt thou commit adultery (Deuteronomy 5:18).

Today, adultery is considered such a harsh word by many that it is seldom used, even by preachers. We speak of "affairs of the heart," "indiscretions," and "sexual liasons."

No matter how softly we try to describe it, adultery still means a married person having sex with someone other than his or her spouse — and the Bible says that is sin!

Jesus broadened the definition of adultery when He said it was not limited to sexual contact, but could also be committed in the heart.

Ye have heard that it was said by them of old time, Thou shalt not commit adultery: But I say unto you, That whosoever looketh on a woman to lust after her hath committed adultery with her already in his heart (Matthew 5:27-28).

110

8. The Bible plainly says:

Neither shalt thou steal (Deuteronomy 5:19).

I think God must have had in mind the thousands who report incorrectly to the Internal Revenue Service when He wrote *Neither shalt thou steal.* The leaven of the Sadducees reasons, "I can cheat the government and not pay them the legal amount I owe because, after all, they waste so much of my money."

That is not what God says.

And Jesus answering said unto them, Render to Caesar the things that are Caesar's, and to God the things that are God's (Mark 12:17).

Jesus did not add, "Unless, of course, they are not good money managers. In that case, you don't have to pay."

"Do not steal" means to give an honest day's work for an honest day's wage. Some Christians expect God or the local trade union to miraculously promote them, regardless of their work ethic. Work hard with God as your employer, and ask Him to bless the work of your hands.

The Lord shall open unto thee his good treasure, the heaven to give the rain unto thy land in his season, and to bless all the work of thine hand: and thou shalt lend unto many nations, and thou shalt not borrow (Deuteronomy 28:12).

For promotion cometh neither from the east, nor from the west, nor from the south.

111

But God is the judge: he putteth down one,
and setteth up another (Psalm 75:6,7).

If we could only get the leaven of the Sadducees out of the work ethic of America, we would surpass our foreign competition in factory productivity. America was founded on hard work, and it is time to get back to a hard day's work for a day's wage.

We need a return to Bible basics in this nation.

At one time, major employers wanted to hire Christian employees because they were honest, they showed up on time when scheduled for work, and they gave a fair day's work for a fair day's wages.

I have heard far too many employers say, "We try not to hire Christians anymore because they show up late for work, take long breaks, and act like the world owes them some sort of a living."

The leaven of the Sadducees steals the precious commodity of time from their employers because they believe in a god of their own invention who covers all their mistakes "under the blood" and requires no accountability.

Get it out. Root out the leaven.

God wants us to be accountable ... to be a people of our word ... to give a day's work for a day's pay.

9.   The Bible plainly says:
Neither shalt thou bear false witness
against thy neighbour (Deuteronomy 5:20).

Why is it that gossip and ugly rumors are so much a part of the Church today?

Because we are cooking with leaven!

A Church free of "false witnesses" is a place of warmth, comfort, security and trust. To the hurting and downtrodden, the Church should represent a sanctuary of safety, a spiritual hospital that specializes in healing — not hurting — those in desperate need of the love of God.

10.   The Bible plainly says:

Neither shalt thou desire thy neighbour's wife, neither shalt thou covet thy neighbour's house, his field, or his manservant, or his maidservant, his ox, or his ass, or any thing that is thy neighbour's (Deuteronomy 5:21).

Root out the leaven of lust and there will be no more pornography hidden in the homes of our ushers, no more "swimsuit issues" on the coffee tables of our preachers, no more "pay-for-view" movie channels bringing their filth and lust into our homes.

This is one of the most violated commandments in our generation and in the Church.

Do we covet the position of another?

This commandment not only deals with possessions, but with our materialistic appetite for titles, promotions, recognition, for being "lifted up" above our neighbor in our jobs, our service in the church, or our social standing in some service club.

Such is the leaven of the Sadducees.

113

Lord, Forgive Us

God, forgive us of the idolatrous sin of presumption, for trying to mold you into a god that fits our conceptions, rather than the God who created the universe.

Lord, put back in our hearts a reverence for your Word, and a deep appreciation that we must seek out our own salvation in fear and trembling before you.

Work out your own salvation with fear and trembling (Philippians 2:12).

Stop taking the word of some preacher over the Word of God!

Stop taking the word of some denomination over the inspired Word of the Bible.

Stop taking the word of some intellectual when we have the holy Word of God Himself!

Tear down the golden calves and believe God is who He says He is.

Rebuke the devil, rooting out the leaven of the Sadducees that picks and chooses which mandates of God to obey, that twists the truths of God's Word, that mistakenly believes they can be conveniently altered to fit self-serving agendas.

On Understanding Darkness

The world is out of control.

Having the understanding darkened, being

114

alienated from the life of God through the ig-
norance that is in them, because of the blind-
ness of their heart: Who being past feeling
have given themselves over unto lasciviousness,
to work all uncleanness with greediness
(Ephesians 4:18,19).

The Sadducees dominate our Church today.

The Sadducees say, "Yes, I know divorce is wrong, but I have a good reason. My wife is a lousy housekeeper, and never has my clothes ironed when I need them. Besides, she doesn't like sex that much anymore. I know God does not want me to put up with this garbage any longer."

The Sadducees reason, "I honestly believe God will not consider it a sin if I look at pornographic magazines once in a while. After all, it stimulates my sex life with my wife."

The Sadducees reason, "Sure, I go to the bar sometimes, but I bet if Jesus lived in my neighborhood, He'd probably go there for a few beers Himself."

The Sadducees are a sad sign of our times.

And then shall many be offended, and
shall betray one another, and shall hate one
another. And many false prophets shall rise,
and shall deceive many and because iniquity
shall abound, the love of many shall wax cold
(Matthew 24:10-12).

Because of their unwillingness to accept and act upon what the Word of God clearly says, the Sadducees fall into the trap of the devil, and have released iniquity in abundance into the cities.

Well, God has a new city in mind for those who get the leaven out of their lives.

The New City

We are going to a city where there will be no crack cocaine babies to weep over. There will be no tenement buildings. There will be no homeless to shed tears for. There will be no ambulances, no insurance companies, no destruction by fire, no sickness, no aspirin, no morphine, no sedatives for sleep.

God will bring the gift of peace to a new city, the new Jerusalem, the city of the great King. No second-class citizens will live there, and the diluting leaven of the Sadducees will be a thing of the past.

And God shall wipe away all tears from their eyes; and there shall be no more death, neither sorrow, nor crying, neither shall there be any more pain: for the former things are passed away (Revelation 21:4).

God will wipe the tears away from families ravaged by divorce; He will take away the sorrow of child-abuse victims; He will erase the grief of families victimized by gangland shootings.

And he carried me away in the spirit to a great and high mountain, and shewed me that great city, the holy Jerusalem, descending out of heaven from God, Having the glory of God: and her light was like unto a stone most precious, even like a jasper stone, clear as crystal (Revelation 21:10,11).

A new Jerusalem is coming, where the glory of God will shine upon all who will get the leaven out. For believers to dwell in the new Jerusalem, all leaven must be eliminated.

And there shall in no wise enter into it any thing that defileth, neither whatsoever worketh abomination, or maketh a lie: but they which are written in the Lamb's book of life (Revelation 21:27).

The leaven will be gone. There will be no abominations, no lies, and no defiling of the sacredness of each and every child of God.

Instead of the city we know today — a city of abuse, addiction and seduction — it will be a glorious city of divine service to the eternal King!

He that overcometh shall inherit all things; and I will be his God, and he shall be my son (Revelation 21:7).

And there shall be no more curse: but the throne of God and of the Lamb shall be in it; and his servants shall serve him (Revelation 22:3).

117

Do you see it?

As we stay faithful and overcome the leaven, we will inherit a NEW CITY, the new Jerusalem.

We will live in a city without curses, and we shall serve Him.

Jesus has clearly declared, *Beware of the leaven of the Sadducees (Matthew 16:6).*

The world has declared you should formulate your own idea of who and what God is.

The choice is yours — to believe the words of men or the Words of God.

We have people who do not believe Jesus is alive today.

Don't listen to them!

"Oh, but, I thought we were supposed to be nice to everyone." We have been too nice for too long!

We have held hands with the world, and it is time to let go, to look the devil in the eye and rebuke him, to pull him down from his deadly throne, and to exalt the name of Jesus Christ!

Beware of the leaven of the modern day Sadducees — they deny the supernatural. They do not believe in the resurrection, or in the gifts of the Holy Ghost.

Beware of the leaven of the modern day Sadducees — they do not believe in heaven or hell or the Ten Commandments.

Beware of the Sadducees.

They are so sad.

We believe in the Holy Ghost; the supernatural; the resurrection of the dead; and the demonstration of the gifts of the Holy Spirit: tongues and interpretation of tongues, prophecy, word of wisdom, word of knowledge, discerning of spirits, wonder-working faith, working of miracles, and healing.

We believe in and commission angels; we believe in demons, and know we are victorious over them.

We are real, bona fide, tongue-talking, devil-stomping, Christ-exalting warriors, attacking the very corridors of hell! Stop eating the leaven of the Sadducees.

Jump out of the puddle and get in the flood.

Behold, I and the children whom the Lord hath given me are for signs and for wonders in Israel from the Lord of hosts, which dwelleth in mount Zion (Isaiah 8:18).

We are a Church given to the world to exalt Him with signs and wonders! We are a Church destined to dwell with Him on Mount Zion.

It is time we started acting like it ... stirring up the gifts within us ... fanning the fires of revival in our hearts ... making ourselves ready as the bride for the bridegroom.

New Age Guides

The Sadducees of our day are declaring this is a "new age" where men and women around the world are coming together in a collective oneness. The gods of all religions are being blended into one great big cosmic melting pot, and we think we can plunk in a soup spoon and dish out whatever god we want for the moment.

Such lies!

We have the only real "spirit guide" in the universe!

New Agers don't need to pay $45 for a few-minute session for someone to channel the spirit world into their homes. What they need is less of the leaven of the Sadducees, and more of the Holy Ghost. Then, they will not need to call upon the spirit world when they have a problem; the Spirit of the living God will be dwelling inside them!

> *But ye are not in the flesh, but in the Spirit,*
> *if so be that the Spirit of God dwell in you.*
> *Now if any man have not the Spirit of Christ,*
> *he is none of his. And if Christ be in you, the*
> *body is dead because of sin; but the Spirit is*
> *life because of righteousness (Romans 8:9,10).*

When the Holy Spirit of God is dwelling in us, we have the power to put down our pornography, our drugs and our alcohol. The Holy Spirit births the desire to worship God instead of money or football. He gives us the boldness to invite unsaved family and friends to receive Jesus. He gives us the righteousness to love our neighbors.

That Special Journey

The irrefutable demonstration of the most profound

fact concerning the resurrection of Jesus Christ of Nazareth is simple: He is not here. He is risen!

Without the resurrection, Jesus of Nazareth is no more meaningful than Buddha or Confucius.

But the resurrection corroborates that He is, in fact, the undisputed Son of God!

> Concerning his Son Jesus Christ our Lord, which was made of the seed of David according to the flesh; and declared to be the Son of God with power, according to the spirit of holiness, by the resurrection from the dead (Romans 1:3,4).

The most vicious leaven of the Sadducees was that they did not believe in the resurrection.

The leaven of unbelief in the resurrection is still around.

1. One group of modern day Sadducees says, "We believe in the resurrection of Jesus, but we do not believe in that other resurrection. We do not believe in that extraterrestrial journey you say we are going to take someday." They do not believe in the rapture of the Church.

2. Another group of Sadducees cannot believe that the same God who can resurrect from the dead, who can rapture the Church, is ever going to resurrect their dead finances, or their dead joy, or their dead marriage, or their seemingly dead anointing.

No wonder the Sadducees are unhappy!

Jump out of that leaven.

121

Enter into the presence of God.

Read His Word and claim His promises.

Accept God's Word for floundering finances. He has given us the power to get wealth so we can help establish His covenant here on earth!

> *But thou shalt remember the Lord thy God: for it is he that giveth thee power to get wealth, that he may establish his covenant which he sware unto thy fathers, as it is this day (Deuteronomy 8:18).*

We can receive God's words of encouragement when we have no joy.

> *These things have I spoken unto you, that my joy might remain in you, and that your joy might be full (John 15:11).*

A struggling marriage can stand on the plan and purpose of God for two to be spiritually united to form one heart, one mind, and one soul — to be fruitful and multiply.

> *Therefore shall a man leave his father and his mother, and shall cleave unto his wife: and they shall be one flesh (Genesis 2:24).*

> *So God created man in his own image, in the image of God created he him; male and female created he them. And God blessed them, and God said unto them, Be fruitful, and multiply, and replenish the earth, and subdue it: and have dominion over the fish of the sea,*

and over the fowl of the air, and over every living thing that moveth upon the earth (Genesis 1:27,28).

It is time for the Church to declare, "Jesus, we want you to be part of our lives more than we want anything in the world."

Rebuke the devil in every situation.

Claim revival in the Church, and in our lives.

Declare from the housetops...

"Jesus, we are not staying bound up one more day. We will study your Word to show ourselves approved, and we will not change one jot or one tittle. You are God, and we thank you for giving us your Word and your Holy Spirit so that we can grow to know who you truly are. Lord, we repent of having false gods before us, and vow to cleanse the leaven of the Sadducees from our lives. We pray this in Jesus' name, Amen."

CHAPTER FOUR

THE LEAVEN OF THE HERODIANS

And he charged them, saying,
Take heed, beware of the leaven
of the Pharisees, and of
the leaven of Herod.
(Mark 8:15)

The Lord, the Flesh, and Good Ole Harry

Harry Harid was a likeable guy, the sort of fellow everyone wants for a brother-in-law. He was a "good family man," and worked a great sales job that provided a steady income for his wife and two boys.

But on this particular afternoon, Harry's mind was not on sales.

Harry Harid removed his dark sunglasses from his car visor and quickly put them on. He looked around cautiously to see if anyone noticed him as he got out of the car — a good block away from the bookstore.

As he walked down the garbage-littered street, he carefully examined faces as he went, relieved there were no familiar people in this part of town who might recognize him.

"Even though I don't live in this rat-infested section of town," he thought to himself, "a fellow can never be too cautious." He had driven thirty minutes to get to this location just to reduce the likelihood of being recognized.

"You never know who you're going to see," he thought, "and I'd have a tough time explaining what I'm doing this far out of my sales territory on a weekday afternoon."

When Harry arrived at the front entrance of the adult bookstore, he quickly dashed inside, breathing a silent sigh of relief that he did not recognize any of the other patrons poking around in the shelves of sordid books and videos.

After spending awhile browsing, Harry finally made his selection of a magazine that graphically depicted, in full color, his favorite form of pornography. Harry took his prize to the cashier, careful to pay in cash so the wife would never see the bill on the credit card receipt. He congratulated himself for his extra-cautious approach, reasoning that "if the wife ever found out, it would just kill her."

Harry then took his magazine from the store in the plain white plastic bag so thoughtfully provided by the porn store. He briskly walked back to the car, feeling much more comfortable now. After all, the risky part was over.

He opened the car trunk and carefully picked up some loose carpeting far away from the tire well and placed his treasure underneath the carpeting, being careful not to create a bulge.

Then, he neatly put the carpeting back, confident that his wife would never discover his hiding place.

"Even if the wife gets a flat tire," he thought to himself, "there's no need for her or anyone else to lift up this carpeting. The jack isn't even close to this carpet, so I'll be okay."

Satisfied that he had covered all of his bases, Harry Harid got into his car and headed toward home.

He had to hurry through the rush-hour traffic.

After all, it was already 5:15 p.m., and he still had a lot to do. There would be the usual dinner with his wife and two kids, and then, since it was Wednesday night, they would all change and rush off again.

Wednesday evening church service started at 7:00 p.m., and Harry needed to get there a bit earlier than most of the others since, on this particular evening, he was one of the assigned ushers.

"Good ole" Harry always prided himself for being such a faithful worker in the church.

Love not the world, neither the things that are in the world. If any man love the world, the love of the Father is not in him.

For all that is in the world, the lust of the flesh, and the lust of the eyes, and the pride of life, is not of the Father, but of the world.

And the world passeth away, and the lust thereof: but he that doeth the will of God abideth for ever (1 John 2:15-17).

The leaven of the Herodians is the spirit of the world, the lust of the flesh, the lust of the eye and the pride of life.

King Herod loved the world.

He was an unscrupulous, crafty, immoral, cruel, lustful, deceitful, cunning and murderous man. Because of his licentious living, Herod was eventually afflicted with a loathsome disease, accompanied by fever. Josephus, the Jewish historian, describes it as...

"An intolerable itching over all the surface of his body, and continual pains in his colon, and dropsical tumors about his feet and an inflammation of the abdomen ... and a putrefication ... that produced worms. Besides which he had a difficulty of breathing upon him, and could not breathe but when he sat upright, and had a convulsion of all his members."[1]

Herod had absolutely no moral integrity, and was ruled by the spirit of lust. The Bible reports that he even married his own brother Philip's wife, Herodias. When the marriage was scheduled to occur, John the Baptist boldly advised the king that he was violating the laws of God in this matter, and told Herod that the Word of God clearly forbade him from marrying his sister-in-law.

For John said unto him, It is not lawful for thee to have her (Matthew 14:4).

Herod married Herodias despite God's law and despite the warnings of the prophet, following instead the worldly lust of his flesh.

On Herod's birthday, the daughter of Herodias danced for him, and her seductive prancings greatly enticed him.

But when Herod's birthday was kept, the daughter of Herodias danced before them, and pleased Herod. Whereupon he promised with an oath to give her whatsoever she would ask (vv.6,7).

Now in the days of Herod, a man's oath was his bond, even if that man were loathsome enough to steal his brother's wife! So, when Herod promised the dancing stepdaughter *whatsoever she would ask*, he was bound to fulfill that promise, no matter what she might request.

To Herod's shock, the stepdaughter, who had been prepared for this opportunity by Herodias, asked for the head of John the Baptist on a platter!

And she, being before instructed of her
mother, said, Give me here John Baptist's head
in a charger (v.8).

Herod was sorry he had made the oath when he heard the stepdaughter's cruel request. Nevertheless, he was bound to honor his oath.

And he sent, and beheaded John in the
prison. And his head was brought in a charger,
and given to the damsel: and she brought it
to her mother (vv.10,11).

Is it any wonder that Jesus warned His followers about the leaven of the Herodians?

And he charged them, saying, Take heed,
beware of the leaven of the Pharisees, and of
the leaven of Herod (Mark 8:15).

Herod Rejected Jesus

Jesus called Herod and his followers hypocrites, and told His disciples to be on the alert for their devious schemes, and to be on a vigilant look-out for their "leaven." At one point, the Herodians tried to trick Jesus by asking Him,

Tell us therefore, What thinkest thou? Is
it lawful to give tribute unto Caesar, or not?
(Matthew 22:17).

Jesus, knowing their intentions, defeated their attempts

to trick Him by answering,

> *Render therefore unto Caesar the things*
> *which are Caesar's; and unto God the things*
> *that are God's (v.21).*

Jesus wanted His followers to be prepared to frustrate the evil intentions of Herod and His other enemies who would bring false accusations of sedition against Him, and try to arouse the people against His ministry.

On the last day of Jesus' earthly life, He appeared before Herod, who openly discredited Him. Herod publicly mocked Jesus by clothing Him in a regal garment before sending him back to Pilate.

> *And Herod with his men of war set him at*
> *nought, and mocked him, and arrayed him in*
> *a gorgeous robe, and sent him again to Pilate*
> *(Luke 23:11).*

The Herods of the 90's

The leaven of the Herodians is so abundant in today's society and in today's Church that it is difficult to tell where the world ends and the Church begins.

If we miss our daytime *soaps*, we can find the condensed plot in our local newspaper. They won't print my sermons, but they will print this garbage.

In 28 minutes and 50 seconds, here is what happened on just one episode:

"Adam gloats over the fact that he has won back his home. Tom leaves Barbara after she confesses that she is

132

carrying Travis' baby. Travis tells Erica that he is the father of Barbara's baby. Erica storms out after Travis lies that he and Barbara conceived the baby by artificial insemination. Billy, who has decided to get rid of Tad in an explosive way, kills Ricky when Ricky does not get the needed material in time."[2]

Adulteries ... murders ... all in 28 minutes and 50 seconds!

We will not murder, but we will watch murder and violence take place daily on our television sets and in the movie houses.

We stay away from adultery, but we will watch it and read about it in the media ... allowing that same spirit of adultery to infiltrate our lives. So why are we surprised when these adulterous thoughts are transferred into adulterous actions ... when we give Satan an open door into our lives?

We will not curse, but we will pay God's tithe money to go sit in some dark theater and listen to someone else do it for us.

The divorce rate among Christians is the same as that in the world. Fifty percent of all married Christians are walking into the divorce court every year, leaving lonely little leaguers and cheerless cheerleaders in the treadmill and garbage heap of their parents' selfish lust.

Five times in one week I received phone calls from wives of preachers who reported that their husbands were out sleeping with someone, or were bringing filthy, pornographic material into their homes and watching it — even right after preaching the Sunday service!

Preacher, I am tired of ministering to teenagers calling in on the prayer lines, pregnant and scared, because you haven't told them the truth that sex out of wedlock is a sin.

No one's kids are exempt.

There is something wrong in America.

There is something wrong in the Church.

We stink from the leaven of the Herodians, and it is time that we cleansed ourselves of it.

The leaven of the Herodians — the spirit of the world and the spirit of sexual perversion (the lust of the flesh, the lust of the eye, the pride of life) — is damning the Church and this planet to hell.

It starts so subtly.

So quietly.

Only now are Christians waking up, as if from a long sleep, and suddenly asking, "How did it get so bad? How did such open, blatant sins as abortion, child abuse, homosexuality, prostitution, pornography, alcohol and drug addiction, and gambling become so firmly rooted in our country and in our Church?"

How?

Through the leaven of the Herodians!

Daily, the Church is dying a subtle, sinful death. Like the frog who fails to leap from a pot of water that slowly comes to a boil, we have compromised our values, our integrity and our morality — little by little, degree by degree, until we are dying in a polluted cauldron.

Herodians in the Media

In 1952, the National Association of Broadcasters established a review board for the television industry, pre-screening television programs before they aired to guarantee that anti-social behavior, such as illicit sexual relations and drunkenness, would be filtered out and not presented as desirable behavior in our society.

The system worked for over a decade.

In 1965, the top-rated shows like *Bonanza, Red Skelton, The Lucy Show, Andy Griffith,* and *My Three Sons* all had strong family values.

But in the quest for higher ratings, daytime soaps began to push the limits of what was allowed.

By the mid '70s, censorship had lost most of its power, and programs started to show increasing depictions of sex and violence. Women in skimpy clothing became a familiar sight.

"Sex sells" became the cry of movie and television producers from the mid '70s.

In the '80s the new cry was, "More sex sells more."

Today, there is no longer any serious censorship in television programming or the film industry.

The leaven of the Herodians has totally taken over the loaf.

135

The movie-rating system is meaningless. More and more, the producers are free to portray the kinds of graphic sex and violence necessary to lure a higher audience share.

It is time for the Church to step into her god-given role and exercise her authority in the heavenlies. It is time to draw the line between good and evil, push back the powers of darkness and root the leaven of the Herodians from this world.

The world will continue to be manipulated by the communications media until we begin to bombard the lying and lustful leaven of the Herodians with our arsenal of prayer.

The media is becoming increasingly bound and controlled by the sold-out servants of Satan who will accept no boundaries of decency or morality in their productions.

It is as though King Herod has become Mr. Harry Herod, chief executive in charge of all that is vile, pornographic and lewd in the television and motion picture industry.

Only a few decades ago, it was controversial to show a man and a woman even sitting on a bed together in a film. The censors demanded that if such a scene was depicted, one of the people must keep a foot on the floor at all times!

Today, film makers liberally show extremely explicit sexual acts. They are spurred by a satanic boldness and the lack of a strong moral outcry. So they push ever further in their depictions of every imaginable perversity.

"Oh, Brother Rod, I do not create these movies. What do they have to do with me?"

To permit them is to participate in the process.

To actually pay to view them is to perpetuate and become part of the perversion.

In the media war between good and evil, the weak sheep of the Church, the borderline Christians, the participants in the leaven of the Herodians, are drawn in by the constant lure of sordid entertainment. Their senses are bombarded by every imaginable sexual fantasy and lust.

And, like Herod watching the dancing girl, their carnal nature is pleased and they are snared.

The media is constantly giving the world their message of "Go ahead and join in. We're having fun, and there's no reason why you shouldn't have fun too!"

Even though the AIDS epidemic is out of control, the media almost never mentions or depicts the potential deadly consequences of sexual sin. AIDS is portrayed as a theme in movies only to show the courage and the strength of the hapless victims — never as the consequence of their sinful lifestyle.

In most movies, the public never even gets a hint that AIDS exists. Movie couples continue to jump into bed on their first meeting with no moral questions, and without any apparent concern for any possible infection from AIDS.

Although billions of dollars have been spent, there is still no vaccine, no cure, and not even an indisputably effective treatment for AIDS. Yet the entertainment media pretends it does not exist, just as Herod pretended that no law existed banning him from marrying his sister-in-law.

Estimates of the number of orphans left behind in the wake of the AIDS crisis now numbers as high as 1.8 million victims worldwide![3]

Satan's evil forces must be rejoicing at the ravages this disease has wrought on families and children over the past decade. What better way to cripple a world and prepare for the takeover by the Antichrist than to create a generation of easily influenced orphans?

And where will these orphans receive their knowledge of the world?

Where will they receive the moral and value systems they need to guide their lives if not from television and the movies?

If we do not get the leaven of the Herodians out of this nation and out of the Church, this generation and the next are doomed to death and destruction!

Beware of the leaven of the Herodians.

Examine Your World

This world and all that is in it should mean nothing to us as Christians.

Nothing.

It is time to break our hold with the world.

The world offers only sensuality, sexual impurity, sexual deviancy and immorality.

The world offers a sex-crazed society where perverted rock stars rake in tens of millions of dollars each year as their reward from the devil for leading our youth down a path of destruction.

Preachers respond to questions regarding movie choices for their congregation with a flippant, "Oh, a little bit of flesh never hurt anyone."

Get it out.

It will damn your soul!

Parents, look at the kinds of magazines your children are reading.

Go through every page.

Just because the cover portrays a hot rod car on the outside doesn't mean that is what is on the inside.

Just because it shows a fourteen-year-old on a skateboard on the outside, doesn't mean that is what is on the inside. I picked up one of the skateboard magazines recently and looked through the first ten pages. I thought, "My God in heaven, no wonder America's youth are on a roller-coaster ride to hell!"

All kinds of demonic symbols and sexual innuendos were in that magazine.

Get the leaven of the Herodians out!

"Well, I don't want to offend my little Johnny by taking away his magazines."

You offend his precious soul when you allow him to keep them on his shelf!

139

"We do not want little Susie to think we lack confidence in her, so we let her have a steady boyfriend even though we know she's way too young. After all, everyone at her school's doing it."

Ask God to Cleanse You!

The leaven of the Herodians hinders our judgment.

Quit ignoring it! It won't go away! It must be driven out by the cleansing water of the Word of God.

Illicit sex will please ... for a moment.

Pornographic magazines will please ... for a moment.

Sin has gratification ... for a moment.

But hell lasts ... for eternity!

Get the leaven out.

For what shall it profit a man, if he shall gain the whole world, and lose his own soul? (Mark 8:36).

Wash the Mud Off

This planet is cursed.

You cannot get a rose without a thorn.

I was standing by our back door as my wife finished mopping the kitchen floor when I looked up to see Ashton, our four-year-old, come running from the back yard. She was covered with mud and heading straight for the kitchen and disaster.

140

I grabbed her just in time. As I scooped her up in my arms, I said, "Wait here, baby. Daddy is going to wash your feet before you go inside."

I ran some water in a bucket and we sat down on the back porch. I then proceeded to wash the mud off her little feet. I dried them with a big towel, and she gave me a big kiss before I let her go.

"Now it's all right," I said. "Now you are clean, and you can go in the house."

Though we are in this sin sick world, we are not of this world. We do not have to stay knee-deep in the mud and muck of the world.

We can be cleansed of the mud of this world through the washing of the Word and the cleansing blood of Jesus.

Let Jesus cleanse the mud from your life.

It is time to get the leaven out, to break our hold with the world.

It is time we realized that God said,

Wherefore come out from among them, and be ye separate, saith the Lord, and touch not the unclean thing; and I will receive you, and will be a Father unto you, and ye shall be my sons and daughters, saith the Lord Almighty (2 Corinthians 6:17,18).

Not many preachers preach this message anymore, and that is why the leaven of the Herodians has crept into the Church.

That is why we are constantly following up on our

141

new "converts," trying to shepherd them back into our pews.

We are not preaching the living of a separated life.

Just as the Jewish fathers of old went through the house cleansing it of all leaven, so must we now go through our own lives, searching our hearts, challenging ourselves to live pure and holy before God.

Love not the world, neither the things that are in the world. If any man love the world, the love of the Father is not in him.

For all that is in the world, the lust of the flesh, and the lust of the eyes, and the pride of life, is not of the Father, but of the world.

And the world passeth away, and the lust thereof: but he that doeth the will of God abideth for ever (1 John 2:15-17).

This whole planet is cursed.

You cannot stay out in the sunshine without getting burned.

There are only two kingdoms.

There is the Kingdom of God and the kingdom of the devil. They are diametrically opposed, and we cannot flirt with one or we will hate the other. That is the reason some people cannot stand church. They have one foot in the Church and the other foot in the world.

I am tired of Christians saying, "How close to the world can I get and still be saved?"

I would rather hear someone say, "How far away

from the world can I get and still be walking around on this planet?"

The World in the Church

Have you noticed?

Our music sounds more and more like the rock bands of the world.

The dresses and suits in our padded pews look more and more like those from the latest fashion show.

Our speech, our topics of conversation, the movies we watch cannot be distinguished from those of the world.

Our divorce rate matches that of the world, and our rate of alcoholism and drug abuse would probably turn out to be about the same if such statistics were available.

John Osteen once said the world has become so churchy and the Church so worldly, it is hard to tell the difference.

God is calling for a great exodus.

God is calling for the Church to come out of bondage.

God is calling for the Church to come out from among them and be separate.

I beseech you therefore, brethren, by the mercies of God, that ye present your bodies a living sacrifice, holy, acceptable unto God, which is your reasonable service.

And be not conformed to this world: but

be ye transformed by the renewing of your mind, that ye may prove what is that good, and acceptable, and perfect will of God (Romans 12:1,2).

God is calling the Church not to touch the unclean thing.

God is calling the Church to be sanctified from the world, to hate the world and all that is in it!

We must draw that John 10:10 line:

The thief cometh not, but for to steal, and to kill, and to destroy: I am come that they might have life, and that they might have it more abundantly.

Anything that blesses our flesh, we say comes from God; and anything that hurts our flesh, we say comes from the devil.

"Well," you say, "Pastor Rod, I know what life is."

No, we think we know what it is. We think it is a perfect body, a Madison Avenue suit and a Wall Street bank account.

Jesus said, "You want to live? I will show you. Come on and die."

Verily, verily, I say unto you, Except a corn of wheat fall into the ground and die, it abideth alone: but if it die, it bringeth forth much fruit. "He that loveth his life shall lose it; and he that hateth his life in this world shall keep it unto life eternal (John 12:24,25).

144

Do not misunderstand God's intention here. Jesus wants us to die to the power of the things of the world, to come out of the world, but that does not mean we should not have material possessions. The Church should have the best there is on this sin-sick planet.

What Jesus does ask is that we not focus our eyes on the material possessions of this world.

I am wearing a little band of gold around my finger. What it symbolizes — my sacred marriage and my beautiful wife — means the world to me. But the gold itself has no meaning in my life.

God, separate us.

Give us young people who will look like God's kids, talk like God's kids, and act like God's kids.

Instead of asking, "What fellowship does light have with darkness?" it is time we start asking, "What fellowship could the devil possibly want with us?"

As tongue-talking, on-fire, Bible-believing, Holy Ghost-filled children of almighty God, we shouldn't look, smell or taste good to the devil. Once we have been inundated with an infusion of the Word of the living God, covered with the blood and filled with the Holy Ghost, we become anointed Holy Ghost powerhouses against the kingdom of darkness!

It is time for the Church to shed the leaven of the Herodians and be refreshed by the soul-cleansing blood of Jesus Christ, the blood of the Lamb.

Put on spotless garments ... white as freshly fallen

snow ... garments repugnant to the devil, and eternally pleasing to our God.

Miraculous Contact

John Lake was a missionary in Central Africa when an epidemic of bubonic plague broke out in one of the villages where he was ministering.

Hundreds upon hundreds were dying; it was one of the most contagious outbreaks that area had ever known.

The government sent a ship with supplies and a corps of doctors. One of the doctors asked him what he had found to inoculate himself with against the virus that was wiping out this village.

John Lake answered, "Brother, that is the law of the Spirit of life in Christ Jesus. As long as I keep my soul in contact with the living God so His Spirit is flowing into my soul and body, no germ can attach itself to me."

The doctor apparently didn't believe him, so Lake proposed he conduct a simple experiment. "Go over to one of these dead people and take the foam that comes from their lungs after death. Put it under the microscope, and you will see masses of living germs. You will find they are alive, but I can put the foam in my hand and the germs will die instantly."

His instructions were reluctantly followed.

"What is that?" they questioned in amazement.

Lake answered, "That is the law of the Spirit of life in Christ Jesus. My spirit and my body are so filled with the blessed presence of God, it even oozes from my pores."[4]

The germs had come in contact with the Holy Ghost repellent of a life lived and dedicated totally to God, a life that repelled the force of darkness!

Light repels the leaven of the Herodians and drives it back.

It is time the Church stopped walking in the world, and stopped being fearful of the world.

Fear God, not the devil.

And then shall that Wicked be revealed, whom the Lord shall consume with the spirit of his mouth, and shall destroy with the brightness of his coming (2 Thessalonians 2:8).

Do you see it?

The Word will consume the enemy!

Brightness shall destroy the darkness, and the leaven of the Herodians will be no more!

CHAPTER FIVE

THE LEAVEN OF THE CORINTHIANS

It is reported commonly that there is
fornication among you,
and such fornication as is not so much
as named among the Gentiles....
(1 Corinthians 5:1)

There was an air of excitment in Felecia's heart that night. After all, it was the night the visiting prophet would be ministering at her church, and she believed God would have a special word just for her!

As the evening service began, Felecia and the rest of the church were not disappointed. God's grace seemed to flow mightily as person after person was set free by the Holy Spirit in that service.

While the prophet was in the process of ministering to one lady in the congregation, he suddenly stopped and began to talk to Felecia and her husband.

"Your husband has cancer," he began, standing over both of them. Since neither Felecia nor Michael had said anything to the prophet about this matter, they both quickly realized that the Lord was ministering through this man, and they both broke into tears. The prophet continued to minister God's Word to Felecia and Michael.

"Satan has launched this attack against you. He will try to take the life of your husband unless you resist this cancer. It is not God's will for this man to die of this disease. In the name of Jesus, I break the power of the ugly spirit of death over this man."

The next day, Felecia called the church, asking to talk to "the prophet of God." Pastor Mark received the phone call.

"What is it, Felecia?" he asked.

"It is about the prophecy we received last night," she replied. "I really do need to talk to the prophet."

"Well, Felecia, I would like to encourage you to share your concerns with me. After all, I am your pastor, and part of my responsibility is to help you with confirmation and counsel regarding words from others."

"Well, okay," Felecia reluctantly agreed. She then shared with the pastor how she had felt in her own spirit that her husband was going to die soon, thus contradicting the word from the prophet.

"Do you want me to respond to that, Felecia?" Pastor Mark asked.

Without hesitating, she said, "Yes!"

With a gentle boldness, Pastor Mark began to share from his heart. "If God told you that your husband was going to die, and then, through the prophet, said it was His will for him to live, then either one of two things has happened. Either God is confused, or one of the words you received was wrong. Since God cannot be confused or wrong, then that only leaves you or the prophet as potentially wrong."

He paused for a minute, then continued,"Jesus came to give life, not death. The Bible says that the thief [Satan] comes to steal, kill and destroy.

"Felecia, I believe the word last night was spoken to destroy the spirit of death that came to you through Satan at that retreat. In His mercy, God imparted the spirit of life, not death, over your husband. Since the prophecy was not incorrect, that means the word you received concerning your husband was wrong, and not instituted by God."

Pastor Mark was not trying to be unkind in pointing out Felecia's deception, but he felt a strong leading of the Lord to be very honest with her. If the lie of this spirit of death was not renounced, the word of life, or the spirit of life would not come to pass over her husband.

"Pastor, I believe you are right," Felecia finally replied, yielding to both the authority of her pastor and to the prophet. After all, Pastor Mark knew her spiritual makeup better perhaps than anyone else on the planet.

After several more minutes of talking with Pastor Mark, Felecia hung up the phone, convinced that she should rebuke the spirit of death and yield to the word from God.

In obedience to the word from the prophet, for the next four months Felecia and her husband waged a mighty spiritual war against the cancer until the doctor finally declared his body "cancer free."

THE LEAVEN OF THE CORINTHIANS

The city of Corinth was known in biblical times as a town of gross immorality. It was the "happening" city, much like Los Angeles or New York City today. Because it was the leading commercial city in Greece, the city symbolized licentiousness and wanton luxury, so much so that the word *Corinthian* is defined by Webster as "a merry profligate man, completely given up to dissipation and licentiousness."[1]

The leaven of the Corinthians was far worse in magnitude and frequency than the leaven of the Herodians. Their excessive sensuality was partly the product of Corinthian worship, particularly of Aphrodite, their goddess of love and beauty. There was even a temple dedicated solely to the worship of Aphrodite!

Of course, being a heathen city, Corinth had many other temples to various gods and goddesses.

Because the excessive immorality of the city overflowed to the Corinthian church, Paul felt it necessary to rebuke the Corinthian congregation in his letters...

It is reported commonly that there is fornication among you, and such fornication as is not so much as named among the Gentiles, that one should have his father's wife (1 Corinthians 5:1).

The person Paul was referring to at the end of this verse apparently took his father's wife as a sexual partner (whether it was his mother or stepmother is not clear). This man was a Christian.

Paul urged the congregation to expel this man until he repented.

> *For what have I to do to judge them also that are without? do not ye judge them that are within?*
>
> *But them that are without God judgeth. Therefore put away from among yourselves that wicked person (1 Corinthians 5:12,13).*

He continued his rebuke of the man who slept with his father's wife in the following verses:

> *And ye are puffed up, and have not rather mourned, that he that hath done this deed might be taken away from among you.*
>
> *For I verily, as absent in body, but present in spirit, have judged already, as though I were present, concerning him that hath so done this deed,*
>
> *In the name of our Lord Jesus Christ, when ye are gathered together, and my spirit, with the power of our Lord Jesus Christ,*
>
> *To deliver such an one unto Satan for the destruction of the flesh, that the spirit may be saved in the day of the Lord Jesus (1 Corinthians 5:1-5).*

Over a period of time, this man was apparently convicted by Paul's words in his first letter, since in Paul's second letter to the Corinthians he urged the congregation to kindly forgive and comfort this man because he had apparently repented.

> *Now I rejoice, not that ye were made*
> *sorry, but that ye sorrowed to repentance: for*
> *ye were made sorry after a godly manner, that*
> *ye might receive damage by us in nothing*
> *(2 Corinthians 7:9).*

The leaven of immorality was ravaging the city of Corinth.

Paul knew the only solution to rooting out the leaven in their midst was to instruct the Corinthians to keep their bodies under subjection by focusing on the eternal rewards at the end of life's race.

The Isthmian Games were held near Corinth, so the Corinthians were well acquainted with athletic contests. Paul therefore wrote to them in examples they could easily understand:

> *Know ye not that they which run in a race*
> *run all, but one receiveth the prize? So run,*
> *that ye may obtain.*
>
> *And every man that striveth for mas-*
> *tery is temperate in all things. Now they*
> *do it to obtain a corruptible crown; but we an*
> *incorruptible.*
>
> *I therefore so run, not as uncertainly; so*
> *fight I, not as one that beateth the air:*
> *But I keep under my body, and bring it into*

subjection: lest that by any means, when I have preached to others, I myself should be a castaway (1 Corinthians 9:24-27).

Paul urged the Corinthians to keep their bodies as if they were preparing for a grueling race — under the same kind of subjection, the same tight requirements, restraints and disciplines.

Judging from the reputation of the city of Corinth, many failed to heed that soul-saving advice.

Corinth Hated Authority

The Corinthians were also sorely lacking in respect for authority, and they refused to accept discipline. They did not want to listen when Paul started to share scriptural mandates for their lives. The Corinthians wanted to be "foot loose and fancy free," and to "do their own thing."

Paul responded to their rejection of authority by reminding the Corinthians that they needed men of God to be their leaders, because no man could govern and be wise without God.

For the wisdom of this world is foolishness with God. For it is written, He taketh the wise in their own craftiness.

And again, The Lord knoweth the thoughts of the wise, that they are vain (1 Corinthians 3:19,20).

Paul asked the Church at Corinth the same question

156

Isaiah had asked the rebellious Jews:

> *For who hath known the mind of the Lord,*
> *that he may instruct him? But we have the*
> *mind of Christ (1 Corinthians 2:16).*

Paul was writing to the various spiritual leaders in Corinth, who in Paul's absence had become influential and self-important, trying to seize control of the Church. They were haughty, overbearing and boastful. Paul responded to these men by once again placing importance not on man's learning but on being God's man.

> *For I know nothing by myself; yet am I not*
> *hereby justified: but he that judgeth me is the*
> *Lord (1 Corinthians 4:4).*

He further warned them to guard against haughty attitudes, and against the belief that their thoughts were somehow greater than God's thoughts:

> *Not to think of men above that which is*
> *written, that no one of you be puffed up for one*
> *against another (1 Corinthians 4:6).*

A bit further along in the same letter, Paul pens one of the strongest arguments ever written against following the wisdom of men and rejecting the authority of God's men:

> *For the kingdom of God is not in word, but*
> *in power (1 Corinthians 4:20).*

He Who Self-governs is a Fool

The undisciplined, unsubmitted leaven of the

157

Corinthians rejects all authority and runs rampant in our churches today.

Across the land, pastors hear the same statements from their flocks.

"I am my own judge. Nobody tells me what to do. I will go to your church ... but the minute you start to meddle in my life, I am not listening to you anymore, and I am moving on."

"I tithe where I feel led. My sister-in-law needs some financial help, so some months I give my tithe to her. And I help out with the pee-wee baseball snack shack fund; I count that as part of my tithe."

"I don't believe I need to go to church on Sunday to be a good Christian. I spend time with my wife, or sometimes I go visit a friend. Sometimes I go for a hike and commune with nature. I believe God honors that just as much as if I went to church, probably more."

On and on the self-deception goes.

There is no place for the leaven of the Corinthians in the Church of Jesus Christ. We are never going to learn to respond to the direct authority of God until we learn to respond to the indirect authority God has placed over us.

If we cannot hear the voice of God through a man of God — and respond to that voice as if God spoke directly to us, then we are never going to be able to clearly hear the voice of God for ourselves. Of course, it is vital we know God's Word for ourselves so no man can lead us astray. The Bible instructs us to try the spirits to see if they be of God.

Beloved, believe not every spirit, but try the spirits whether they are of God: because many false prophets are gone out into the world (1 John 4:1).

Just Agree With Me!

Today, it seems we all want to act like we know everything, and everyone else is wrong but us.

We need to understand that we do not respect authority because that authority is right.

We respect authority because it is the authority!

Authority can be wrong, but it must still be respected!

Thinking we know everything that is right and everything that is wrong has become a primary problem in the Church today. That type of thinking was at the root of Adam and Eve's trouble in the Garden of Eden.

Adam and Eve had no respect for authority.

Most of the people sitting in churches today have no respect for spiritual authority. If we do not like the way we are disciplined, we just puff up like toads and go somewhere else down the road ... until they offend us. Then we puff up like a toad again and go on down the road.

That's the truth.

Once and forever, why not nail our feet down somewhere? Why not make a commitment? Why not say, "In the name of Jesus, God placed us in this church. This is our church, and let the gates of hell try to prevail against

159

us. This is our church and we are going to stay here and serve Him!"

When I was young, the teachers were always right.

Today, everyone seems to think that the teachers, the principals, the administrators and the department heads are all wrong. We think everyone is always wrong but us, because we refuse to submit to authority.

If we come under authority, especially as we pray for those who lead us, we will experience a quiet and peaceable life.

I exhort therefore, that, first of all, supplications, prayers, intercessions, and giving of thanks, be made for all men; for kings, and for all that are in authority; that we may lead a quiet and peaceable life in all godliness and honesty (1 Timothy 2:1,2).

Remember the rewards God promised when we honored the authority of our parents?

Honour thy father and thy mother, as the Lord thy God hath commanded thee; that thy days may be prolonged, and that it may go well with thee, in the land which the Lord thy God giveth thee (Deuteronomy 5:16).

Conversely, when we do not honor authority, we come out from under the covering of God, and subject ourselves to the curses of the enemy.

Stop correcting and confronting those in authority and worrying about matters that have nothing to do with you. If you are not in a position of responsibility, then God does not require accountability from you in that area.

Our primary responsibility is to make it to heaven. We are responsible for doing everything under our power to see to it that we get there, but we are not responsible for the other matters, so there is no use in worrying about them.

Stop worrying about those who have authority over you. They will answer to God for their actions — not you.

Wake Up!

The Church is baking in the leavened bread of the Corinthians, and we are becoming love-hate Christians.

When we first come to church, we love everything. We love the music, the choir, the preaching and the nursery. We exclaim, "There is no place like this on the face of the earth! This must be the place for me because there is no other place around like this."

Oh, we love everything until we have been there about two weeks.

Then we hate the choir that we used to love; we hate the ushers; we hate the nursery.

We are love-hate Christians, incapable of a sustained, harmonious relationship.

Unruly People

Too many Christians are not willing to accept church

161

discipline. They do just fine as long as the church is giving to them, but when the church begins to require something from them, then the rules change.

We want responsibility, and we love the church as long as the church does not also demand accountability.

"Pastor, my wife and I just can't accept your decision that we should stay together. We have talked about it, and we sincerely feel that we should divorce. We can still serve God as singles."

We refuse to allow God's men to rule over us!

Yield to spiritual authority.

Find your place in the Church, function in that place and bear fruit, bringing increase to the body of Christ.

Most people who come to the church offices for personal ministry do not want to hear the truth. They come looking for someone to agree with the decision they have already made! When the person in authority does not agree with the decision they have already made, they turn and leave in a huff, rejecting the counsel they have received.

The truth is, we need to pray and rebuke the devil's deceptions.

Why do we need to talk about the problem over and over when we have the answer?

We can answer every need with one word: Jesus!

People get angry with me all the time when they seek my counsel because they have already made up their minds about what they are going to do. Young couples come to me for premarital counseling and announce, "Well, we have decided to get married."

I may say, "You made the wrong choice."

"What do you mean we made the wrong choice?" they ask, shocked at my words.

"Have you talked to any spiritual authority over you about this union?" I ask.

"No, no. God told us!" they proudly respond.

I have nothing else to say at that point.

After all, I am not God. I am not above God.

"If you say God told you, well, that just zips my lips. I'm done. There's no need for my counsel."

People always make their decisions first, and then want God and His men of authority to bless them.

Why not ask God and His men in authority to bless us BEFORE we make these life-changing decisions?

I have had young people sit right in front of my desk in my office and ask, "Don't you think we should be married?"

I say, "No, I do not."

So they get up, very angry, and march off to another church and find another pastor to perform their wedding ceremony.

Then, two years later, they are divorced.

I have to tell many of these young couples who want to be married, "Number one, do not ever come back in this office again until you make a covenant commitment before me and before God that you will stop sleeping

163

together. Don't walk in here and ask me to bless what God has cursed. I cannot bless what God has cursed."

So often, when I ask the question, "What do your parents think about the person you are marrying?" I hear comments like, "They think she is too immature." "They think he is all right, but they think we should wait."

What "they think" makes no difference to the youth of our generation. We live in a generation that has no respect for any authority.

This generation is full of the rebellious leaven of Corinth. It is time to repent of the leaven of the Corinthians, and yield to the authority God has placed over us, calling on Him in prayer to guide us and bless our counsel.

Immorality and Fractured Families

Because of the gross immorality in society today, our families are fractured and dying. Billy Sunday once said, "In view of eternity, how can one allow a moment of adulterous pleasure to separate one from God?"

We need help.

One of the downfalls of this nation is the divorce court, producing fractured families that are not genetically linked, producing men who have young girls in their homes who are not of their blood.

Make no mistake about it.

This is an open door for demonic activity; and unless

it is slammed shut, the devil will come racing through it!

We have *your* kids, and *my* kids, and *their* kids, and *our* kids, and they are all living together under the same roof. When mom and dad go out for the evening, they leave little fourteen-year-old Alice home with little fifteen-year-old Johnny.

They have no blood barriers between them. This is an open door for the devil to lure these children into sexual temptation!

You say, "Well, does that always happen?"

No, it does not happen when you get the leaven of the Corinthians out!

Give the devil no place in your home; don't give him a doorway of opportunity.

The number one way to slam the door in the devil's face is to stop divorce, to kill the lie that, "Things will be better just as soon as I get rid of that no-good spouse."

Things usually get worse.

Next, teach your children to make life choices.

This day I call heaven and earth as witnesses against you that I have set before you life and death, blessings and curses. Now choose life, so that you and your children may live (Deuteronomy 30:19, NIV).

Get the leaven of the Corinthians out.

Just as in the Old Testament days, rooting out the leaven starts in the home.

Respect for authority starts in the home.

165

Children need to understand the chain of command in the home, with the father at the head and the mother at his side.

The chain of command was specified by God, so every time we step out of that chain of authority we are in trouble, and that kind of trouble breeds rebellion.

There is a rebellion that was bred in this nation in the early 1960s that today we accept as normal.

Even in our Christian school, parents are constantly coming into the office telling us their child has a detention when he did nothing wrong. If the parents have no respect for authority, then the children are not going to have any respect for authority.

Parents, teach your children respect for authority.

Teach them words like *mister, ma'am,* and *sir.*

Teach them words like *thank you* and *please* and *excuse me.*

Respect for authority — it is God's way, and God's rule.

Parents, as you teach your children respect for authority, show them, by example, how a person in authority under God walks in the ways of the Lord.

Train up a child in the way he should go,
and when he is old he will not depart from it
(Proverbs 22:6).

In the midst of the constant violence and negatives in television and the movies, let them see their authority figures doing the things of God in their lives.

Let them see and experience charity, encouragement,

nurturing, obedience to God's will, and a deep concern for the needs of others.

Let the family unit reflect God's authority, starting with the relationship of the husband to the wife.

Wives, submit yourselves unto your own husbands, as unto the Lord.

For the husband is the head of the wife, even as Christ is the head of the church: and he is the saviour of the body.

Therefore as the church is subject unto Christ, so let the wives be to their own husbands in every thing.

Husbands, love your wives, even as Christ also loved the church, and gave himself for it;

That he might sanctify and cleanse it with the washing of water by the word,

That he might present it to himself a glorious church, not having spot, or wrinkle, or any such thing; but that it should be holy and without blemish.

So ought men to love their wives as their own bodies. He that loveth his wife loveth himself.

For no man ever yet hated his own flesh; but nourisheth and cherisheth it, even as the Lord the church (Ephesians 5:22-29).

Do you see it?

Godly authority governs in godly love, nourishing

167

and cherishing those who are governed, just as God nourishes and cherishes us and the Church!

If husbands and wives are to live as an example of Jesus, then in the family unit they will covenant to love, care for, nurture and cherish each other.

Husbands are called of God to be loving leaders, providers and malice protectors. Wives are called to be nurturers and cooperative partners. Both are called to esteem and respect each other.

> *Nevertheless let every one of you in particular so love his wife even as himself; and the wife see that she reverence her husband (Ephesians 5:33).*

God commands all who are in authority to be ready to forgive and to radiate the love of Jesus in our relationships with others.

> *Finally, be ye all of one mind, having compassion one of another, love as brethren, be pitiful, be courteous:*
>
> *Not rendering evil for evil, or railing for railing: but contrariwise blessing; knowing that ye are thereunto called, that ye should inherit a blessing (1 Peter 3:8,9).*

Corinthian Malice

The Corinthians hosted many evil thoughts toward Paul, often holding malice against him. Malice is an evil thought life, and it is part of the leaven of the Corinthians.

I had a good friend who was an ex-Hell's Angel. His fists were as big as my thighs. He weighed 275 pounds, and stood about 6'6". After he was born-again, he was one of the gentlest men I ever met.

But not so in his unsaved days!

He told me about being in a bar one night when someone walked by and touched his girlfriend in an obscene manner. He followed that man into the restroom, pulled out a gun, pinned the man up against the wall and shot him in both knees.

I once heard him say, "I have stolen. I have shot men. I have stabbed men," he said. "But you know the only difference between me and you? I did what you thought."

The Church today is full of malice, full of evil thoughts of envy, of hatred, of backbiting and whispering. We smile at people to their faces and then sit in church and talk about them behind their backs.

Out of the same mouth proceedeth blessing and cursing. My brethren, these things ought not so to be (James 3:10).

We are full of cursing.

We might just as well rip open our corrupted hearts and expose the filthy rags of our own righteousness.

The body of Christ does not know how to control its tongue.

169

Behold, we put bits in the horses' mouths, that they may obey us; and we turn about their whole body.

Behold also the ships, which though they be so great, and are driven of fierce winds, yet are they turned about with a very small helm, whithersoever the governor listeth.

Even so the tongue is a little member, and boasteth great things. Behold, how great a matter a little fire kindleth!

And the tongue is a fire, a world of iniquity: so is the tongue among our members, that it defileth the whole body, and setteth on fire the course of nature; and it is set on fire of hell (James 3:3-6).

We need to bridle our tongues so that we do not sin before God.

I said, I will take heed to my ways, that I sin not with my tongue: I will keep my mouth with a bridle, while the wicked is before me (Psalm 39:1).

Today's atmosphere is so hostile that when a preacher is attacked by the press, the Church, instead of circling the wagons to protect one of their own, begins throwing the stones to finish him off!

A good man out of the good treasure of the heart bringeth forth good things: and an evil man out of the evil treasure bringeth forth evil things.

170

But I say unto you, That every idle word that men shall speak, they shall give account thereof in the day of judgment.

For by thy words thou shalt be justified, and by thy words thou shalt be condemned (Matthew 12:35-37).

Following the instructions of the apostle Paul, bridle your tongue and get the malice out of your heart.

Finally, brethren, whatsoever things are true, whatsoever things are honest, whatsoever things are just, whatsoever things are pure, whatsoever things are lovely, whatsoever things are of good report; if there be any virtue, and if there be any praise, think on these things.

Those things, which ye have both learned, and received, and heard, and seen in me, do: and the peace of God shall be with you (Philippians 4:8,9).

God wants us to DO good things, to dwell on pure, holy, lovely things, things of good report. As we do, there will be no room for malicious thoughts in our minds. Decide today to live the life of God rather than the lies and deceit of the enemy.

God tells us to be kind.

A soft answer turneth away wrath: but greivous words stir up anger (Proverb 15:1).

God encourages us to be gentle.

*A wrathful man stirreth up strife: but he
that is slow to anger appeaseth strife (Proverb
15:18).*

God encourages us to be merciful.

*The merciful man doeth good to his own
soul: but he that is cruel troubleth his own
flesh (Proverb 11:17).*

God encourages us to walk in His name, giving
thanks in all we do. If we do that, there is no room for
the leaven of malice to exist in our lives.

*And whatever you do in word or deed, do
all in the name of the Lord Jesus, giving thanks
to God the Father through Him ... And whatever you do, do it heartily as to the Lord and
not to men (Colossians 3:17,23).*

Finally, we need to pray and ask God to help us practice the biblical principles He has given us to walk in and
to reflect His love. Cast out the leaven of malice that
permeates much of the Church today.

*Love suffers long and is kind; love does not
envy; love does not parade itself, is not puffed up;
does not behave rudely, does not seek its own,
is not provoked, thinks no evil; does not rejoice
in iniquity, but rejoices in the truth; bears all
things, believes all things, hopes all things, en-
dures all things. Love never fails (1 Corinthians
13:4-8).*

No Fruit

The Corinthians were heavy on the gifts and light on fruit. Everyone wants to talk in tongues, prophesy, preach, work miracles, manifest the gifts of healing; but so few are willing to pay the price of living according to God's mandates.

Scripture warns us to guard against...

Envyings, murders, drunkenness, revellings, and such like: of the which I tell you before, as I have also told you in time past, that they which do such things shall not inherit the kingdom of God (Galatians 5:21).

In light of Jesus' teaching in Matthew 15:18, murder in this passage is better interpreted "destroyer of another's happiness" rather than "physical" murder.

But those things which proceed out of the mouth come forth from the heart; and they defile the man (Matthew 15:18).

How many times have we murdered?

How many times have we been responsible for destroying someone's joy?

How many times have our tongues filleted a preacher on the way home from church?

Stop it!

Her ways are ways of pleasantness, and all her paths are peace (Proverb 3:17).

Let God cleanse our thought lives and our motives.

173

Trust in the LORD with all thine heart;
and lean not unot thine own understanding.

In all thy ways acknowledge him, and he
shall direct thy paths (Proverb 3:5,6).

If we are only on the platform to sing and be seen, then we don't need to be there.

If we are only in church to perform, then we need to take our performance where it belongs. Performances belong in the world, not in the church. The Church is not a place of performance; it is a place of humble worship.

Preachers, stop expecting someone to escort you in and escort you out. Get into the midst of the people. Feel their hurt, and let their needs be your needs.

Jesus said,

And he said unto them, The kings of the
Gentiles exercise lordship over them; and they
that exercise authority upon them are called
benefactors.

But ye shall not be so: but he that is
greatest among you, let him be as the younger;
and he that is chief, as he that doth serve
(Luke 22:25,26).

I am tired of Corinthian preachers who make better actors than they do prophets of God.

I am tired of preacher-businessmen who would do better on Wall Street than in the holy sanctuary of God.

Get the malice out, cleanse the leaven and make way for a Holy Ghost revival.

174

And that we may be delivered from unrea-
sonable and wicked men: for all men have not
faith (2 Thessalonians 3:2).

"Lord, deliver the Church from wicked and unreasonable men" is the cry of my heart.

Wicked people aren't hard to spot.

If we are born-again, Holy Ghost-filled, fire-baptized, tongue-talking, devil-stomping believers on our way to heaven, then we know that running around with a pimp is associating with a wicked person.

A drug dealer is a wicked person.

Everyone can identify the openly wicked people.

But unruly and unreasonable people are a little harder to identify. They are slippery creatures ... people who are incapable of maintaining a sustained, harmonious relationship.

You and I know some people like that.

When we see them, we have no earthly idea what part of that person we are going to meet. We walk on eggshells around them because we never know how they will react in a given situation. It could be wrath today and smiles tomorrow.

They are unruly people, incapable of a sustained, harmonious relationship.

Why?

Because relationships take work.

If you are going to love me, it is going to take some work. Anyone can love me when I am lovable, but to love

175

me when I am unlovable, the way Jesus loves me ... that takes some work.

> *But I say unto you, Love your enemies, bless them that curse you, do good to them that hate you, and pray for them which despitefully use you, and persecute you;*

> *That ye may be the children of your Father which is in heaven: (Matthew 5:44,45).*

Through the grace of God, we can cleanse ourselves of an unruly spirit and of a wicked thought life! The Living Bible makes the entire matter of Godly living very clear and simple:

> *Is there any such thing as Christians cheering each other up?*

> *Do you love me enough to want to help me?*

> *Does it mean anything to you that we are brothers in the Lord, sharing the same Spirit?*

> *Are your hearts tender and sympathetic at all?*

> *Then make me truly happy by loving each other and agreeing wholeheartedly with each other, working together with one heart and mind and purpose.*

> *Don't be selfish; don't live to make a good impression on others.*

> *Be humble, thinking of others as better than yourself.*

*Don't just think about your own affairs,
but be interested in others, too, and in what
they are doing.*

*Your attitude should be the kind that was
shown us by Jesus Christ, who, though he was
God, did not demand and cling to his rights as
God, but laid aside his mighty power and
glory, taking the disguise of a slave and becoming like men.*

*And he humbled himself even further, go-
ing so far as actually to die a criminal's death
on a cross (Philippians 2:1-8, TLB).*

I see a day coming when the world will look at
Christians and cry, "I want what they have. I want to be
like they are. They love each other so deeply, they serve
each other so willingly. I want to experience that kind of
relationship, that kind of joy in my life."

I see a day coming when even the world will see the
sharp distinction between the mud and mire of the
Corinthians and the might and glory of the redeemed.

I see a day coming when we will reflect and radiate
the bright light of a Church totally transformed by God's
love, a light that will attract the world to our door, begging us to teach them what God has shown us.

I see a day coming when the leaven of the
Corinthians — gross immorality, malice, backbiting, and
lack of respect for authority — will be as repugnant to us
as they are to God.

I see a day coming when we will be a cleansed Church, a bride ready for the bridegroom, purified by God's transforming grace.

Yet, while we remain on this earth, I see us being the ministers of the Gospel God intended for us to be: His ambassadors and servants with hands to minister to a hurting and dying world who desperately needs our blessed Savior.

I see a day coming when those in the world will come to us desperately seeking to find those things that they have never experienced, anxious to be what we are — reflections of the Christ who dwells within us.

CHAPTER SIX

THE LEAVEN OF THE GALATIANS

*So Christ has made us free. Now, make sure
that you stay free and don't get all tied up
again in the chains of slavery to Jewish
laws and ceremonies.
(Galatians 5:1 TLB)*

"Honey, Why Do You Love Me?"

As Mike reached over to turn off the light by the bed, his wife of twenty-nine years asked him a rather unusual question.

"Honey, why do you love me?" she asked.

Now Mike had been married to Karen long enough to recognize when she was joking and when she was serious, and tonight, she was asking a serious question.

Still, Mike needed clarification. He could not quite believe Karen had asked the question at all.

"Why do I love you?" Mike asked in as steady a tone as possible, trying hard not to be sarcastic. "Honey, I'm not quite sure what you mean. Surely after twenty-nine years of marriage, you know why I love you."

"Well, sometimes it is just nice to hear. Please, tell me what I do that makes you love me."

Mike recognized this was not a time to be funny or cute. Karen was indeed serious, and for whatever reason, she wanted to actually hear from his lips the words and the feelings in his heart.

"Well, let's see. Honey, I love you because you are such a giving person. You are so anxious to reach out to our children and give them whatever they need — a hug, a bowl of hot cereal in the morning, a bandage for their cuts — you are just always there for them."

Mike paused.

"Go on," Karen encouraged, snuggling a bit closer

to Mike. "Tell me more."

"Well, I love the way you put those little love notes in my lunches, and the way you greet me with such warmth when I come home at night."

"Go on, tell me more."

"You know the way you laugh? That giggle that reminds me of the little kid in the television commercial? I love that."

Mike was beginning to feel a bit frustrated. How could he possibly tell Karen all the things in his heart? How could he possibly reduce to mere words the deep inner bursting of joy and affection he had for his precious wife?

"Oh, honey, this is so hard," he said. "There are just so many things about you I love, so many things you do, so many things you say that make me glad you are my wife, that make me happy. I just can't begin to re- duce them to a few sentences."

"Try," Karen replied, wrapping her arms around Mike's chest. "I love to hear it. Please, tell me more."

"Okay," Mike began. "Let's see... Oh, I know, I love the way you minister to the women in our church who are hurting. Every time you receive a phone call, every time we go to church, it's as though the faces of the other women light up and shout, 'Hey, Karen's here. She loves me, and she will listen to my deepest hurts.' Honestly, in a way, honey, I'm almost jealous how much others love you because they know you love them so much."

"That's so sweet," Karen replied, wiping a small tear from her eye. Inside her heart of hearts she was beginning to get the message that she was indeed loved. But somehow, she felt there was something else she needed to hear, but did not know quite what it was. Still searching, she asked, very gently, one more time.

"Is there anything else? Any other reasons?"

By now Mike was a bit clearer in his own mind how he felt, and he responded.

"Yes, there is. Honey, most of all, I love that whole totality that makes up you. Your smile, your giggle, your heart, your cute little figure, the mole on your cheek, the one foot that is a bit larger than the other — I love every bit of you. I love you, not just when you are doing things for me or the kids or the women at church, but when you are doing absolutely nothing. I love you in the morning when you are sitting in your chair, reading your Bible. I love you in the afternoon when you are just sitting on the couch taking your afternoon break. And sometimes, I think I love you the most when I creep into bed late at night and you are already asleep, just being still.

Honey, my love for you does not depend on what you do — it is because of who you are — Karen, my wife, my love, the person I cherish more than any other out of the five billion people on this planet. There are no conditions. There's nothing you have to do. You have my love, period. I guess, when all is said and done, I just love you because you're you."

That hit the inner core of Karen's heart.

Her quest for answers was over on this particular night.

Nodding her head ever-so-gently as it rested on Mike's chest, she responded, "That's nice. That's really nice. Thank you. Good night."

THE LEAVEN OF THE GALATIANS

The Galatians attempted to justify their relationship with God by the works of their flesh.

Many of the citizens of Galatia were converted Jews, and attempted to establish their own righteousness through the Mosaic Law instead of the "righteousness due to faith" provided by the New Covenant.

Paul responded to them by writing:

Knowing that a man is not justified by the works of the law, but by the faith of Jesus Christ, even we have believed in Jesus Christ, that we might be justified by the faith of Christ, and not by the works of the law: for by the works of the law shall no flesh be justified (Galatians 2:16).

The congregation of the Church at Galatia were a mixture of Jews and Gentiles. Many converts from Judaism still scrupulously kept the ceremonies and other obligations of the Mosaic Law, insisting on circumcision and other requirements of the Law as necessary components of salvation.

These enemies of truth kept the circumcision issue alive even after the apostles and other elders in Jerusalem had dealt with the matter.

Paul wrote plainly against this false teaching:

And that because of false brethren unawares brought in, who came in privily to spy

185

out our liberty which we have in Christ Jesus,
that they might bring us into bondage
(Galatians 2:4).

Like the Sadducees and the Pharisees, the Galatians opposed God's man, and tried to discredit Paul as an apostle. They wanted the Christians to be circumcised, thinking this would pacify the Jews, and keep them from opposing their congregation so violently. The Galatians were trying to avoid suffering persecution for Christ.

As many as desire to make a fair shew in
the flesh, they constrain you to be circumcised;
only lest they should suffer persecution for the
cross of Christ (Galatians 6:12).

The Galatians argued that circumcision would profit the church at Galatia, and that it would advance them in Christianity. They claimed that through the act of circumcision, they would be true sons of Abraham, to whom the covenant of circumcision was originally given.

Paul thoroughly refuted the contentions of these false Christians and built up the Galatian brothers so they would stand firm in Christ.

He told them,

Christ hath redeemed us from the curse of
the law, being made a curse for us: for it is
written, Cursed is every one that hangeth on a
tree: That the blessing of Abraham might come
on the Gentiles through Jesus Christ; that we
might receive the promise of the Spirit through
faith (Galatians 3:13,14).

186

The message Paul gave to these battling Galatians is a message that needs to be heard today by the modern-day, too often legalistic, Church:

Stand fast therefore in the liberty where-with Christ hath made us free, and be not en-tangled again with the yoke of bondage.

Behold, I Paul say unto you, that if ye be circumcised, Christ shall profit you nothing.

For I testify again to every man that is cir-cumcised, that he is a debtor to do the whole law.

Christ is become of no effect unto you, whosoever of you are justified by the law; ye are fallen from grace (Galatians 5:1-4).

Just One More Deed

The leaven of the Galatians is our attempt to justify our worthiness, or relationship with Christ, through the works of the flesh.

"I'm going to heaven because I never fail to go to church on Sunday, and I sing in the choir."

"Lord, you love me because I say the rosary every single day."

"Lord, you love me because I work with these homeless people down at the food center each Wednesday afternoon."

"Lord, you love me because I visit the sick at the nursing home and bring them flowers."

187

On and on it goes.

Anything we do out of routine that does not flow spontaneously from our hearts toward God is religion — the work of the flesh.

Cast out any dependance on good works for acceptance by God.

God has a much better plan, called "Grace," and it is a FREE GIFT from Him.

For all have sinned, and come short of the glory of God;

Being justified freely by his grace through the redemption that is Christ Jesus (Romans 3:23,24).

"You started off in the spirit," Paul said, "but then you entered into this works' dogma. You cannot earn your way to heaven."

"Works" is not just counting beads on a rosary. Anything can become dead, lifeless and religious that separates us from a true relationship with God. I use the word *religious* to describe anything that becomes repetitious and mechanical in our worship, devoid of the freshness of the Spirit of God. Those things we do out of routine, and not from a heart hungry for God, are works of the flesh.

Shouting His praises can become religious.

Loud singing, clapping and dancing can become religious.

Quiet, soft songs can become religious.

Jumping up and down can become religious, and

standing solemnly can become religious.

Folding our hands and bowing our head to pray can become religious; kneeling down to pray can become religious.

We do not need to labor under "works" any longer. God loved us so much that He gave us Himself, and that is all the "work" that needs to be done.

I am going to heaven because I believe on the Lord Jesus Christ with all my heart, mind, soul and strength. I believe in my heart and confess with my mouth that Jesus Christ of Nazareth, the only begotten Son of God, came down from heaven, died on a rugged cross, and shed His blood for the justification of my sins.

I believe He rose again from the dead for my justification, went back to the Father, and sent down the Holy Ghost who fills my life. I believe He is imminently returning again to receive me because I accepted the propitiation, the price paid for my sin — the redeeming, forgiving, life-giving blood of Jesus Christ of Nazareth.

When Christians first begin their walk with the Lord, they all believe what I believed when I was first saved, and still believe.

But then, they gradually fall into a works mentality that allows the devil's condemnation to come in, because they cannot ever work hard enough or long enough to "justify" their eternal salvation.

The Nature of Grace

G stands for gift, the principle of grace.

R stands for redemption, the purpose of grace.

A stands for access, the privilege of grace.

C stands for character, the product of grace.

E stands for eternal life, the prospect of grace.[1]

Grace is the free gift of God; there is nothing we can do to earn it.

> *For by grace are ye saved through faith;*
> *and that not of yourselves: it is the gift of God*
> *(Ephesians 2:8).*

If there is nothing we can do to earn it, then there is nothing we can do to keep it. And if there is nothing we can do to keep it, and there was nothing we could do to earn it, when we fall short in the flesh, we do not lose it — it is still operative.

When we sin, we have an advocate, an attorney in heaven. We have Jesus Christ, the righteous, pleading our case with the Father!

We do not receive grace by signing someone's church roll.

We do not receive it by going to church and sitting on the front row.

You do not have any more of it than I do, and I do not have any more of it than you do.

It is the free gift of God.

Talk about love!

Talk about mercy!

God loved us in the depth of our sin. Are we going to act like He does not love us now?

If He loved us then, He can surely love us now.

"He loves me!"

This is the greatest defense against the onslaught of hell, the greatest defense against the lie that says, "You are not DOING enough for God, so your salvation is in question."

"God loves me."

Period.

His grace is a free gift.

Redemption is the purpose of grace. To redeem means to return to the original state of affairs.

Christ hath redeemed us from the curse of the law (Galatians 3:13).

In the mind and heart of God, every human being on this planet is already forgiven. Even the person in the deepest depth of sin is forgiven, if he will only ask to receive the forgiveness of God.

If Adolph Hitler would have decided to kneel down and cry out to God, he could have received forgiveness. Even though he had instigated and overseen the death of over six million Jews, he could have been forgiven — because God's grace is unlimited, without measure!

So many of us accept the lie that we cannot be forgiven. That is not God's plan.

When Jesus said *It is finished* on that old rugged cross, it was forever finished in the mind and heart of God.

191

Jesus says, "It is finished, and forgiveness is yours. If you had an abortion, you can be forgiven. If you are on your fourth marriage, you can be forgiven. If you abused your child, you can be forgiven. No matter what crime, no matter what offense you have committed, my love is greater than your offense, and you can be forgiven if you will repent and receive me as the propitiation for your sins."

When Jesus rose from the dead, His resurrection meant we were justified. We are justified by Jesus — NOT by our works!

If there had been any sin that was able to separate us from the love of God, Jesus would still be in the tomb, paying the price.

If Jesus had not shed His blood to forgive the sins we are entangled in right now, if God the Father had not forgiven us for every sin we have ever committed up to this very moment, if the price had not been paid ... Christ would still be in that tomb.

But on the third day, He arose from the dead, victorious over death, hell and the grave, and the Father said, "It is enough! It is enough! The price is paid for every human being that will ever draw a breath of air on this earth! I have forgiveness enough for every single one, and it flows through my freely-given grace."

Gypsy Smith tells the story of an atheist who placed an ad in his local newspaper that proclaimed on a particular Sunday he was going to stand out in a field and curse the name of God and damn God's name.

If there was a God, he reasoned, fire would come down out of heaven and destroy him.

At 2:00 in the afternoon, the atheist went out to that field and started yelling and screaming at God, swearing every oath he could swear. He screamed at the heavens until he was red in the face, his veins protruding in his neck.

Finally, in exasperation, he told the crowd, "See, I told you there was no God."

An old lady just waved her hanky and said, "Excuse me, Sir. What you have proven today is that God is who He says He is. He is the giver of all grace, and His grace has been extended to you today. You have proven that God is who He says He is. His grace is inexhaustible, and you are still alive to prove it."

You cannot get away from it.

Grace will wake you up in the middle of the night saying, "Let me in, let me in."

"No, I do not deserve to have you come in. I am bad, ugly, mean. I am a vile, cruel sinner."

We do not knock on the door of God!

Jesus said,

> Behold, I stand at the door, and knock: if any man hear my voice, and open the door, I will come in to him, and will sup with him, and he with me (Revelation 3:20).

That is grace.

We do not have to locate Him ... He is looking for us!

Redemption is the purpose of grace, to return us to the original state of affairs — as clean as Adam and Eve were in the Garden of Eden before they sinned. That is how clean His grace washes our blackened hearts.

Access is the privilege of grace.

Through Calvary's bleeding Lamb, we can get from where we were through the veil that was torn in two in the Holy of Holies. He gave us access into the very throne room of God where we find grace to help us in time of need, where we cry, "Abba, Father."

For through him we both have access by one Spirit unto the Father (Ephesians 2:18).

Just imagine.

The Holy God, the Creator of the universe, gives us free access into His presence!

We do not need to come into a building so a man standing behind a podium can give us access into the presence of a holy God.

We do not need to attract the attention of any famous television preacher to have access to God.

The veil that hung in the temple, four inches thick, woven without seam, twenty feet wide and forty feet high, was torn from top to bottom by God, and He said, "I am coming out and you are coming in."

Into God.

Run to God. Never shy away, never hide your face in shame, never shrink back. He has torn the veil, and by His grace we have access.

What a privilege!

Character is the product of grace.

Grace humbles us before God. Humility is the greatest character-building stone known in the arsenal of God, and grace humbles us.

That God would condescend to us, that God would give us access into His presence, that God would forgive us — that a righteous God, the only God, the mighty God, would redeem us — is humbling!

Character is built within us because we know who God is and, therefore, we know who we are.

> *Humble yourselves therefore under the*
> *mighty hand of God, that he may exalt you in*
> *due time (1 Peter 5:6).*

We are humbled at the realization that the only reason we are allowed in the throne room of God is because, though we did not deserve it, Jesus paid our ransom and let us come to the heavenly banquet, free of charge.

"'Come and dine,' the Master calleth, 'come and dine.' You may feast at Jesus' table all the time. He who fed the multitudes, turned the water into wine, to the hungry calleth now, come and dine."[2]

He invites us to His feast.

That is grace.

We can come into His presence.

We cannot come because of our own ability, and that is humbling. We could never climb that mountain. We could never find the key to unlock that heavenly door to enter into the presence of God without grace.

God resists the proud and the haughty.

Why?

Because the proud and the haughty are self-sufficient and self-reliant, and they have no need of God. They go contrary to the very nature of God, which is grace.

When we say, "I can do it on my own," we negate God from being God.

When we say, "God, you are everything and I am nothing," we allow God to be God in our lives.

Grace was there before faith, and grace will be there after faith.

God gives us access to His presence while we are yet dirty, rotten hunks of stinking, sinful flesh. God allows us to come into His holy, pure presence just as we are ... sinners in need of a Savior.

We have the privilege of access to Him because of grace.

<u>Eternal life is the prospect of grace</u>.

The finished work of grace — eternal life — is what we are looking for.

Think of it ... we are going to live forever!

Why?

Because the end product of the grace of God is eternal life. We are alive, never to die, because there is something inside us called "immortality."

Immortality is what separates Christianity from every

other form of religion in the world. It makes it a relation-ship, not a religion, because we are going to live forever in the pavilions of God, walking on streets of gold, hear-ing the angelic song, and marching and dancing to the song of the redeemed throughout the endless ages of eter-nity.

The prospect of God's grace:

If any man believes in Jesus Christ, though he were once dead, yet shall he live (John 11:25).

Eternal life.

We have something to look forward to.

Grace is not finished yet.

We are going to a city whose builder and maker is God, and there we are going to be the kings and priests!

Blessed and holy is he that hath part in the first resurrection: on such the second death hath no power, but they shall be priests of God and of Christ, and shall reign with him (Revelation 20:6).

When we get up there, it will not matter what we were — the President of the United States, the Queen of England, or a used-car salesman.

It does not matter.

We are all going to live on Hallelujah Street and Glory Boulevard. We are all going to walk on streets that are made of gold and live in a "mansion just over the hill-top, in that bright land where we'll never grow old."[3]

The prospect of grace?

Let me tell you what grace is going to do.

Grace is going to a lonely hillside in eastern Kentucky. Up on that little hillside is a grave marked with the name of my uncle who served his country in the rice paddies of Vietnam, and went to be with the Lord at twenty years of age. He went over there with an angelic face, and came back with half of it gone. I am a prospector looking for something everyone said could not be found.

I am on a journey.

I believe the prospect of grace is that one day there is coming a great getting-up morning when graves will open. The dead in Christ are going to rise first, and then we who are alive and remain shall be caught up into the clouds to be with the Lord forever.

It may happen tomorrow afternoon at 2:15 p.m., or it may happen early in the morning at 3:30 a.m.

I do not know when it is going to happen, but I do know this — it is going to happen!

What a prospect!

I am not only going to see loved ones who have gone on before me. The prospect of grace is that I am going to walk past David's restored tabernacle of praise and worship; and I am going to pass by those trees planted on either side of the river of life from which spring the twelve manners of fruit, the leaves of which are for the healing of the nations.

I am going to have the privilege of climbing up

before the Great White Throne of Almighty God, and bowing down before Him. I shall behold the One with the nail prints in His hands, and the nail prints in His feet ... the One with the open side from which came blood and water, that saved a sinner like me.

> *And he shewed me a pure river of water of life, clear as crystal, proceeding out of the throne of God and of the Lamb.*
>
> *In the midst of the street of it, and on either side of the river, was there the tree of life, which bare twelve manner of fruits, and yielded her fruit every month: and the leaves of the tree were for the healing of the nations.*
>
> *And there shall be no more curse: but the throne of God and of the Lamb shall be in it; and his servants shall serve him:*
>
> *And they shall see his face; and his name shall be in their foreheads (Revelation 22:1-4).*

That is the prospect of grace — eternal life, that we are going to live forever.

Receive Salvation

How blessed we are!

Our salvation is not dependent on the length of our skirts, or whether we have stripes on our shirts, or zippers or buttons on our jackets.

Through grace, we can be different. We do not have

199

to be bound up as children of God, forced into molds where we must look like everyone else.

The leaven of Galatia leavens the whole lump.

It makes the whole thing the same. God said He was not going to build His church out of leaven. He was not going to build it out of bricks that all looked the same, that all came out of the same mold.

He is going to build His house with living stones, and He is the stonecutter. He is the One who is going to shape us, and mold us and make us.

As lively stones, are built up a spiritual house, an holy priesthood, to offer up spiritual sacrifices (1 Peter 2:5).

Salvation is by grace.

It is by the blood of the cross of Christ, nothing less and nothing more.

We have become too legalistic in the Church.

How ridiculous it is to point to a man's wedding ring and say, "Brother, that's jewelry, and it can keep you out of heaven. Get rid of it." Yet, the person making that silly declaration is wearing an expensive Rolex watch loaded with diamonds, and tells us "A watch is okay because it is a timepiece, not jewelry."

Oh, men are so foolish!

Men and women should not have to be afraid of eternal damnation because they think their sleeve lengths and skirt lengths are not exactly the right measurements.

We do not need to look like the world or act like the world, but it is time we allow the Holy Ghost of God to give us the dictates of our heart.

When we start telling people the truth about how they can get to God, they will be so hungry to live for God they will shun the wrong and do the right.

They will be like Job. If we will hold up the standard of the cross, they will eschew evil and run to righteousness.

Legalism is a Lie

"Make your confession this way, and everything will be all right."

"Pray this prayer, and here is the outline."

Our pursuit of God must be born out of the deepest desires of our hearts, not out of discipline. We are not walking around like little puppets with someone dictating how we should act.

We are bought with a price, and man did not pay it!

God shed His precious blood on Calvary for us, and He is the only One we need to please!

"What can wash away my sin? Nothing but the blood of Jesus. What can make me whole again?"[4]

Nothing —
 not washing our hands
  not the length of our skirts
   not how we wear our hair
    not the way we stand up
     not the way we sit down
      not the way we pray our prayers —
       but the blood of Jesus.

Come with me to the scene of the crucifixion.

They plait a crown of thorns and pierce it into His brow. The Roman's whip tears the flesh from his back; it hangs in strings from His bones. They kick and prod Him through the cobblestone streets of Jerusalem.

On the cross, He cries, "I thirst," and they give Him vinegar to drink. His muscles tremble under the weight of the curse of our sin. A rivulet of crimson blood streams down His forehead to His brow.

Does He turn His head to keep it from falling?

No.

He drops His head forward and it falls to the ground. It splashes in the dusty, sandy soil of Calvary.

Hear him.

He said, "This drop of blood is for you."

There is only one way to salvation, and that is by the blood of Jesus Christ!

It pays the price. The total price is paid and mankind can be free.

Salvation Versus Legalism

Charles Finney, when asked by one of his professors what he was going to do after law school, replied, "Put out a shingle and practice law."

The professor said, "Then what?"

"Get rich" was Finney's reply.

"Then what?"

"Retire."

"Then what?"

"Die."

Moving his chair up to his desk and pulling his glasses from his eyes, that elderly squire then asked the riveting question, "Then what?"

Finney clasped his head in his hands and ran out and found a place by a stump in the woods and wept his way to salvation. Because, after that riveting question, Finney had only one answer: After that, "The judgment."[5]

Finney experienced the saving blood of Christ in the privacy of the woods, and let that blood change his life.

Like Finney, so many Christians first experience God in their hearts. Then, at some point in their walk, they fall into the trap of legalism — trying to do works to earn salvation.

Do not confuse legalism with the law.

Jesus said,

> *Think not that I am come to destroy the law, or the prophets: I am not come to destroy, but to fulfil (Matthew 5:17).*

Jesus came to fulfill the law.

Trying to perform various works to earn salvation is legalism. Too many Christians mistakenly believe they are made righteous — right with God — by acts or works.

Paul wrote extensively about legalism in the book of Galatians.

> *So Christ has made us free. Now, make sure that you stay free and don't get all tied up again in the chains of slavery to Jewish laws*

and ceremonies. Listen to me, for this is serious! If you are counting on circumcision and keeping the Jewish laws to make you right with God, then Christ cannot save you (Galatians 5:1,2, TLB).

The Covenant Sign

Why does the Bible talk about circumcision?

It is a sign of the covenant.

It is the cutting of flesh and the spilling of blood under the Old Covenant which made the Jews, as much as they could be, in right-standing with God before Jesus died on Calvary.

God said all the sons of Israel were to be circumcised as a sign of covenant relationship.

God never breaks His covenant.

God never alters His covenant.

Some people wonder why the Jewish race seems to be able to show up in any country of the world with nothing more than the will to survive, and within three years they are living in the finest homes in the city, and everything they look at just turns to money.

Ask them why.

They will say, "I am in a covenant with God."

"But, Brother Rod, they are not born-again."

That has nothing to do with the covenant. They are still in a covenant with God.

When a Jewish boy is circumsized on the eighth day

after his birth, the Jews believe that child is entering a covenant with their God.

Are they saved by circumcision?

No!

But God said,

> And I will bless them that bless thee, and
> curse him that curseth thee: and in thee shall
> all families of the earth be blessed (Genesis
> 12:3).

Look at that little expanse of land in Israel. Jesus called the city of Jerusalem the city of peace. Yet no other square footage on the face of this planet has been fought over more, and has had more blood spilled upon it than that little strip of land on the Mediterranean Sea.

It does not matter what their enemies or adversaries do against them — whoever curses Israel is cursed, and whoever blesses Israel is blessed.

God is in a covenant with the Jews, and no one can alter that covenant.

What we have today in Christianity flows out of an understanding of Judaism, and of the Jewish culture. God raised up the Jewish people out of nothing ... He created a nation to bless out of the loins of one man.

He told Abraham,

> In blessing I will bless thee, and in multi-
> plying I will multiply thy seed as the stars of
> the heaven, and as the sand which is upon the
> sea shore; and thy seed shall possess the gate

of his enemies; and in thy seed shall all the
nations of the earth be blessed; because thou
hast obeyed my voice (Genesis 22:17,18).

The congregation at Galatia was composed of many of these Jews who had been nourished and raised in that tradition and heritage. Now, they were having to learn something new, and it was difficult for them.

The New Covenant says Jesus has already been crucified. He has already shed His blood. He has already been raised from the dead. He has already ascended back to the Father. He has already sent the Holy Spirit to the earth.

And these confused Jewish people were still walking around Galatia trying to have favor with God, saying, "I have favor with God because I am circumcised; and you Gentiles are not circumcised, therefore Jehovah will not have anything to do with you."

Paul said, "Wait a minute! This thing is not by works of your religion. Your religious ceremonialism means nothing to God."

What a text for the twentieth century Church!

Paul told them, "Anyone trying to find favor with God by being circumcised must also obey every other Jewish law or perish. Christ is useless if you are counting on clearing your debt to God by keeping laws. You are lost from God's grace."

Paul told them about grace!

What does it mean?

It means God comes to blacks, whites and yellows.

It means He loves the curly-haired ones, the straight-haired ones, and those who do not have very much hair.

It means it is a gift.

In chapter three of Galatians Paul says, "Listen, you started off well. Who brought this confusion? Who be-witched you? Who hindered you? Who did you listen to that led you away from the elementary principle of the grace of God?"

O foolish Galatians, who hath bewitched you, that ye should not obey the truth, before whose eyes Jesus Christ hath been evidently set forth, crucified among you? (Galations 3:1).

Paul knew God is not impressed with long prayers or the offerings we give in church.

God is not influenced by how many church services we attend.

Am I saying we should not pray?

No.

Am I saying we should not attend church?

No.

All these things are according to the Word of God.

Yes, we should give our offerings.

The Bible says,

Give, and it shall be given unto you; good measure, pressed down, and shaken together, and running over, shall men give into your bosom (Luke 6:38).

Yes, we should attend church.

The Bible says,

Not forsaking the assembling of ourselves together, as the manner of some is; but exhorting one another: and so much the more, as ye see the day approaching (Hebrews 10:25).

We do need church.

We do need to go by the Book. There are no new revelations. "Well, I just cannot get along over there at that church, so I just meditate on the Word on my own."

It is right to go to church.

But, if we think we gain favor with God as a result of our actions, then we are confused and deceived.

If we think we receive the grace of God as a result of our actions, then we are no different than those who say "We have to be circumcised," or those who say "We have to carry candles," or those who say, "We cannot wear any jewelry or make-up or we will be sent to hell."

This life is not about works!

We must understand this, getting this truth deep in our spirit, so the depth of our understanding of who God is will increase.

Otherwise, if we are not careful, we will slip into the doctrine of works, feeling guilty because we can "never DO enough." Then we will end up feeling condemned because we have not fulfilled our works.

The devil beats Christians over the head with that rolling pin all the time, and we should stop that lie right now!

Do you know what I told the devil one time? I said, "Here is my Bible, devil. I am saved by the grace of God, and I am not reading it tonight. Good night."

Why?

Because he told me I was not saved, and I would not be right with God if I did not read another chapter that night. So I told him, "Devil, I am not even going to read the one I was going to read, just to prove that God loves me regardless."

Bask in His Grace

When we deny the fullness of God's grace, we limit His presence in our lives.

God's plan of redemption was to return us to the original state of affairs He created in the Garden of Eden.

In Genesis 1 and 2 we learn that God created man in His image, after His likeness. God formed man of the dust of the ground and breathed into his nostrils the breath of life. Adam's eyes popped open and God said, "See all this, son? You are in charge."

The restoration of God's redemptive power into our lives returns us to the power to walk on this planet with authority.

We walk on this planet with ability.

We walk on this planet with anointing.

We walk on this planet with acceptance before God.

Why?

Because of who we are?

No!

Because God laid down a bridge, and when we walked across that bridge, He changed us into who we now are.

Grace! God designed it. We have nothing to do with it. God established grace before He ever created us.

Grace is a godly characteristic, and only the God-life flowing through us can cause it to manifest in our lives. Grace is absolutely of God, and when it does manifest, we should attribute it to God.

It is God's grace when someone loves me when I am unlovable. That person is operating in something beyond themselves.

Paul said in the book of Ephesians,

That at that time ye were without Christ,
being aliens from the commonwealth of Israel,
and strangers from the covenants of promise,
having no hope, and without God in the world:
But now in Christ Jesus ye who sometimes were
far off are made nigh by the blood of Christ
(Ephesians 2:12,13).

Amazing grace took a people who had "no hope," and through the blood of Christ, made us a people who now have the authority, the anointing and the ability to walk on this planet. We who were once alienated from God, separated from Him by sin, we who were contrary to God, are now able to walk with acceptance and favor on this planet in the eyes of God.

It does not matter what we do.

It does not matter if we give our body to be burned, if we sell our houses and give all the money to the poor and walk around barefoot in the middle of January with six inches of snow on the ground, and do it in the name of Jesus — it will not earn our salvation!

It does not matter if we give a cold drink to someone who is thirsty.

We still have no access to God without grace.

We can approach the throne of God and find grace to help in time of need. We can boldly, with confidence (not arrogance), approach God. We can approach the very throne of God and receive what God has.

That is a privilege.

The wall between us and God, erected through sin, has been crushed with a deadening blow by the cross of Christ on Calvary's hill, and we now have access to His presence!

We do not need anyone to take us.

We do not need anyone to go for us.

We do not have to dress right.

We do not have to say the right thing.

God gives us free access into His almighty presence through His grace.

Nothing will destroy the leaven of Galatia quicker than the Church's understanding of the nature and the power of the free gift of grace!

If we are born-again, we have access right into His very throne room.

"My sin — O the bliss of this glorious tho't — My sin, not in part but the whole, Is nailed to the cross, and I bear it no more: Praise the Lord, praise the Lord, O My Soul!"[6]

The devil is telling us, "You cannot go to God. You haven't prayed enough. You haven't read your Bible enough. You haven't witnessed enough."

God is far bigger than our ability to please Him.

One of the most freeing revelations that ever came to my mind was when God spoke in my spirit several years ago and said, "Do not ever try to please me again. I am already pleased."

I said, "Lord, what do you mean?"

He said, "See what I see."

I said, "Lord, I cannot see it."

He said, "See what I see."

I said, "I cannot see it."

He said it one more time, "See what I see."

And suddenly I saw the base of a bloody cross, and God said, "I am pleased."

Do not try to please Him. All we need to do is believe in the finished work of Calvary.

"Jesus paid it all, all to Him I owe. Sin had left a crimson stain, He washed it white as snow."[7]

"At the cross, at the cross where I first saw the light, And the burden of my heart rolled away, it was there by

212

faith I received my sight, And now I am happy all the day!"[8]

"Amazing grace! how sweet the sound, that saved a wretch like me! I once was lost, but now am found, Was blind, but now I see."

"When we've been there ten thousand years, Bright shining as the sun, We've no less days to sing God's praise Than when we first begun."[9]

In the church of my youth, we followed that with a refrain that said, "When the battle's over, we shall wear a crown, we shall wear a crown, we shall wear a crown. And when the battle's over, we shall wear a crown in the new Jerusalem."[10]

The leaven of the Galatians can pollute the whole loaf, and God said He was not going to build His Church out of leaven!

Salvation is by grace.

Salvation comes by the blood of the cross of Christ.

Nothing less and nothing more.

We cannot work our way to heaven.

We cannot earn our salvation through circumcision, or through any other action.

God shed his precious blood on Calvary for us, and the price has been paid.

Period.

CHAPTER SEVEN

THE CLEANSING SOLUTION

For the word of God is quick,
and powerful, and sharper than
any twoedged sword, piercing even to
the dividing asunder of soul and spirit,
and of the joints and marrow,
and is a discerner of the thoughts
and intents of the heart.
(Hebrews 4:12)

"You know, Charlie, it's hard to believe you and Dottie get along so well after all these years. Do you have some sort of secret?" Charlie's neighbor, Donald, asked as he returned the hedge clippers he had borrowed the week before.

"We have a method to our marriage," Charlie replied, putting away the hedge clippers Don had just returned, "but I can't honestly say it is much of a secret."

"What do you mean?" Don asked, very interested, especially since his own marriage to Darlene had seemed to go only downhill these past seven years.

"Is there some sort of course you took, or what? Darlene and I have so much garbage in our marriage I don't think we'll ever get it out. I almost believe it would be best to leave her and start over with a clean slate."

"Know what you mean," Charlie replied. "Once felt that way about Dottie."

"Nooo. You've got to be kidding," Don replied, not believing what he had just heard.

"No, it's true," Charlie replied, picking up a polishing rag and wiping the fender of his '56 Buick while they talked. "After thirteen years of marriage, Dottie and I didn't even like each other. But in our day, you stayed together because of the kids. So, we did. But for our own survival, we decided to seek counseling at our church."

"And that's what got you straight?" Don interrupted, anxious to find a quick fix for his fractured marriage.

215

"Not exactly. Oh, it helped and all; but the thing really didn't start to break until one day when I accepted Jesus into my heart in a real and personal way. Oh, I was a church-going person before, but when I broke down and admitted my life was a mess, and that I couldn't make it work, cried out to Jesus for help, and turned my life over to Him — then things started to change."

"You mean that was all there was to it? You accepted Jesus and things turned around," Don questioned.

"Not exactly. There were things I needed to learn, and when I started reading the Bible, I started to learn them," Charlie responded.

"What kind of things?"

"Basic stuff, really," Charlie answered. "No real secrets. For one thing, I learned that my role as a husband was not to criticize Dottie, but to nourish and encourage her. God intended for me to be her personal minister."

"Oh, boy, that would be a challenge. What would I say to minister to or encourage Darlene? Go shopping? Spend more money? Sleep more than she already does?"

"No, not that sort of stuff. That creates the problem. You see, God designed us like He designed a plant. If you fed the plant poison, what would happen?"

"That's easy, it would die."

"Well, when you gripe and complain to Darlene, you are feeding her poison. It is like putting leaven in unleavened bread. Pretty soon the whole loaf is leavened. You keep complaining, and pretty soon you've killed your plant."

216

"So what am I supposed to do, ignore her faults?"

"Yeah, I suppose so. Most of the time, anyway. When you have a plant and you want it to grow, you only prune it maybe once a year, and only then when it's healthy. The rest of the time you just keep the soil fertilized, water it, treat it real gentle like ... and some folks even talk to their plants."

Charlie paused to put some glass cleaner on the headlights, then he continued.

"That same stuff works pretty good for people too. Of course, if there is a bug that could hurt the plant, you pluck that off real quick. That's because you are the plant's protector."

Don had a huge frown on his face.

"That all just sounds too simple, too basic. And besides, you just don't know Darlene."

"I know her better than this '56 Buick."

"What do you mean?" Don quickly responded, not quite sure what to think.

"Just this. When you put pure gasoline in this baby, it runs just the way it was designed to. Now, you go mixing water in the gasoline and the thing sputters, loses power, and barely makes it out of the driveway.

"The same is true with Darlene, or any other human being. God designed us all to run best on nurturing, on being cherished, on hearing good, positive, true things — things of good report. When we mix that relationship with criticism and bitterness, it is like water in gasoline. Pretty soon, the relationship doesn't work any more."

"That's a lot to think about," Don replied.

Just then, his wife called to him over the fence in a rather urgent-sounding, impatient voice.

"Don, we're going to be late for the pee-wee baseball game if you don't hurry," Darlene said.

Just as Don was about to shout back to her, "I'll be there when I'm ready," he felt a check in his heart. Looking at Charlie, then taking a deep breath, he replied, "You're right, Honey, it is getting late. Thanks for reminding me. I'll be right there."

Darlene had been puffed up and poised for another fight. But when she heard Don's reply, it felt like a soft wind. All she could mumble back, in the midst of her surprise, was, "Okay, honey, I'll go get your leather coat."

The words shocked Darlene as she walked away thinking, "In thirteen years of marriage I have never gotten Don his coat. What made me say that now?"

With a wink and a handshake, Don left Charlie polishing his car.

As he walked back to his own yard, Don thought to himself, "Someday, maybe my marriage can shine as bright as that old '56 Buick in Charlie's garage."

THE CLEANSING SOLUTION

When Rip Van Winkle went up to Sleepy Hollow for his incredibly long nap, King George III was the leader of England. Britain had tight control over the colonies of the United States of America. When Rip left for his nap, he saw, hanging on a shop window, an image of the head of George III.

As the story goes, Rip slept for many, many years.

When he came down from Sleepy Hollow, the image of George III had been replaced with the image of another Englishman by the name of George — George Washington.

Rip Van Winkle had slept through an entire revolution!

Today, much of the Church is about to sleep through a revolution — a Holy Ghost revival that is sweeping and covering the earth like the waters cover the sea.

Wake up!

God does not want us to sleep through it!

For too long we have been believing God for a little trickle of blessing while the flood tide of the glory of God is pouring over the sapphire sill of heaven's gate, and splashing the sides of the earth.

We are living in a day when the Church is about to see the greatest revival in the history of the world; and conversely, the world is about to see the greatest revival in the history of the Church!

Do not miss it.

The kingdom of darkness has been overthrown; the Kingdom of Light is dispelling the darkness.

The power of God is available to all who call upon the name of the Lord.

We are living in the endtime, and it is time for the Church to do what the Church has been called of God to do — preach the Gospel to the entire world.

Our Powerful, Covenant God!

If the Old Covenant had been perfect, there would have been no need to have the New Covenant.

If Adam and Eve had acted according to God's plan in the Old Testament there would have been no need for the New Testament.

But man sinned, creating the need for a redeemer.

If there had been no New Testament ... if Jesus had not gone to Calvary ... we would still be sick, depressed, lonely and discouraged, in despair and desperation ... with no hope!

But Jesus shed His precious blood on a lonely hillside outside Jerusalem called Golgotha.

He went there for you and for me!

The Old Covenant gave us far more power than most Christians realize.

Hebrews 11 gives us a summary of what the saints were able to accomplish — even under the Old Covenant.

Who through faith subdued kingdoms, wrought righteousness, obtained promises, stopped the mouths of lions,

Quenched the violence of fire, escaped the edge of the sword, out of weakness were made strong, waxed valiant in fight, turned to flight the armies of the aliens.

Women received their dead raised to life again: and others were tortured, not accepting deliverance; that they might obtain a better resurrection (Hebrews 11:33-35).

Yet, the Old Testament was limited. It was only a temporary solution until God said, "It is not enough; I will make a new covenant."

God having provided some better thing for us, that they without us should not be made perfect (Hebrews 11:40).

The Old Covenant saints witnessed many mighty miracles at the hand of God.

But today, under the new and more powerful covenant, we think it is a miracle if a fever leaves the brow of one of our children.

They raised their children again from the dead!

They stopped the violence of the sword.

They stopped the mouths of lions.

By faith, *Enoch was translated that he should not see death (Hebrews 11:5).*

By faith, Abraham *went out, not knowing whither he went (Hebrews 11:8).*

By faith, *Sarah herself received strength to conceive*

seed, and was delivered of a child when she was past age, because she judged him faithful who had promised (Hebrews 11:11).

By faith, the Jews *passed through the Red Sea as by dry land (Hebrews 11:29).*

By faith, *the walls of Jericho fell down (Hebrews 11:30).*

God Honors Sacrifice

Under the Old Covenant, there was a great man, a Gileadite named Jephthah. Jephthah was much like us.

Now Jephthah the Gileadite was a mighty man of valour, and he was the son of an harlot: and Gilead begat Jephthah.

And Gilead's wife bare him sons; and his wife's sons grew up, and they thrust out Jephthah, and said unto him, Thou shalt not inherit in our father's house; for thou art the son of a strange woman (Judges 11:1,2).

There is no wrong side of the tracks when we serve God. There is no wrong lineage in God. God creates all men equal in His sight. We may be in the homeless shelter today, but we do not have to be there when the sun pops over the horizon tomorrow.

There is a way out.

His name is Jesus.

The Holy Bible is our book of instructions to understanding the nature of Jesus, and to having a personal relationship with Him. It is the oak of God planted in the forest of eternity, entwining its roots around the Rock of Ages.

It teaches us how to die, and it teaches us how to live.

If the Church is to be free of leaven, we all need to get that nonsense out of our minds that we are the wrong color ... the wrong size ... the wrong shape ... the wrong nationality ... the wrong education.

We are ALL the right color!

"Well, I do not speak the right language,"

Then learn the new language — the Holy Ghost language!

"Well, you do not know what kind of an environment I came out of."

Sixty-five percent of all children of color in this nation are being raised in single-parent homes; and because of that, society wants them to believe that they cannot be anything, or go anywhere — because "everyone is holding me down."

That is not what the Bible says. The Book declares, *If God be for us, who can be against us? (Romans 8:31).*

Let the Holy Ghost go deep down on the inside of our spirit man. Allow His presence to flood us from the top of our heads to the bottoms of our feet.

We are the apex of the creation of God, made in His image, created in His likeness.

Let every man be a liar, but let God be true.

We are a people of destiny. We may not have arrived

at our destination yet, but we are on our way.

Do not listen to the voices of this world. Do not listen to the negative voices all around you. Do not listen to those who would hold you down and keep you back and say you cannot be the person God intended you to be.

Do not eat the leaven of the world, but dine on unleavened bread.

Unleavened bread never spoils!

A preacher friend of mine once said, "When we are full of the Word and full of the Holy Ghost, it makes us feel like we are somebody when we know we ain't nobody."

We do not have to be bound to crack cocaine, or bow our knees to drugs — because *Greater is he that is in me than he that is in the world! (1 John 4:4).*

It is time to get the leaven out of our lives ... to quit hanging around with the devil's deadbeats.

Get away from the places where sin hangs out, and mix with a crowd of God's Holy Ghost believers who know the Book is true, what God said is true, and He will bring to pass everything He promised.

Prayer Power Is Real

Jephthah was determined. When his half brothers kicked him out of his house and took away his inheritance, Jephthah fled to Tob. There he gathered a band of men around him who served under his command.

Later, when the children of Ammon gathered them-

224

selves to make war against Israel, they needed a capable military leader. The elders of Gilead decided to try to fetch Jephthah out of the land of Tob.

> *And they said unto Jephthah, Come, and be our captain, that we may fight with the children of Ammon (Judges 11:6).*

They wanted something he had — military leadership.

They sent for Jephthah, and he said, "I will only lead our people in battle and fight this war if you let me rule in peacetime also."

> *If ye bring me home again to fight against the children of Ammon, and the Lord deliver them before me, shall I be your head? (Judges 11:9).*

They agreed to his terms.

Jephthah gathered mighty men from each of the twelve tribes of Israel except the tribe of Ephraim, which decided not to go out to war with Jephthah. Because of that decision, the war was waged out of balance. Jephthah, the great general, now stood in the middle of the battlefield — outnumbered, outweighed, outmanned and outarmed.

Jephthah realized that unless something supernatural happened immediately, he would surely lose the battle and his life. The armies of Israel would perish, and he would go down in recorded history as a man who failed.

Maybe it was because he was born on the wrong side

of the tracks ... maybe it was because he was the son of a harlot ... maybe it was because his family had thrown him out ... maybe it was because of those difficulties that he had learned not to be a quitter but a fighter, a warrior and a mighty man of valor. In the midst of apparent defeat, something on the inside of Jephthah rose up, and he said, "Wait a minute. I am Jephthah, and I am not going to die on the field of battle. My epitaph is not going to read, 'Jephthah, man of failure.'"

Jephthah sought God. He prayed to God and pledged a vow unto the Lord if God would *without fail deliver the children of Ammon into mine hands (Judges 11:30).*

Seeking God in prayer is a lost art in the body of Christ. We do not know anything about prayer, yet we cannot keep the leaven out of our lives without the protection of prayer.

A renowned divinity scholar once said, "Prayer? Why not use a prayer wheel?"

This man who supposedly knows the Bible is comparing prayer to a spinning wheel of chance like they use on the Wheel of Fortune.[1]

When we take prayer out of the hearts of born-again, spirit-filled believers, when we take prayer out of the hearts of our nation, jerk prayer out of our schools — rip out the very contact with a supernatural God who is able to deliver us out of every situation and give us hope when there is no hope — we cannot hope to make it in this world.

The leaven will spoil the loaf.

Another so-called scholar of the Harvard Divinity school once made the statement, "I do not believe that the religion of tomorrow will have any more need of petition (prayer) than it will have for any other form of magic."[2]

Leaven is even polluting our seminaries!

I may not have as many degrees as these studied men, but I do know how to read, and my Bible says,

> *If my people, which are called by my name, shall humble themselves, and pray, and seek my face, and turn from their wicked ways; then will I hear from heaven, and will forgive their sin, and will heal their land (2 Chronicles 7:14).*

Pray With Urgent Faith

Jesus tells us to have faith in God and in prayer!

> *And Jesus answering saith unto them, Have faith in God.*
>
> *For verily I say unto you, That whosoever shall say unto this mountain, Be thou removed, and be thou cast into the sea; and shall not doubt in his heart, but shall believe that those things which he saith shall come to pass; he shall have whatsoever he saith.*
>
> *Therefore I say unto you, What things soever ye desire, when ye pray, believe that ye receive them, and ye shall have them (Mark 11:22-24).*

227

Have faith in your prayers to God.

Notice, I said "faith in your prayers to God," not faith in your denominations, your local church or a Harvard graduate.

Have faith in God.

God said,

> Call unto me, and I will answer thee, and shew thee great and mighty things, which thou knowest not (Jeremiah 33:3).

The apostle John said,

> And this is the confidence that we have in him, that, if we ask any thing according to his will, he heareth us:

> And if we know that he hear us, whatsoever we ask, we know that we have the petitions that we desired of him (1 John 5:14,15).

And Jesus said,

> And I say unto you, Ask, and it shall be given you; seek, and ye shall find; knock, and it shall be opened unto you.

> For every one that asketh receiveth; and he that seeketh findeth; and to him that knocketh it shall be opened (Luke 11:9,10).

The old hymn writer said, "Sweet hour of prayer, sweet hour of prayer that calls me from a world of care, and bids me at my Father's throne make all my wants and wishes known. In seasons of distress and grief, my soul has often found relief, and oft escaped the tempter's snare by thy return, sweet hour of prayer."[3]

Jephthah said, "I know what I will do. I will pray."

Jephthah did not have much time. The Ammonites and the Moabites were on their way. He could see their swords glistening in the noonday sun. He could hear their hideous war cries like hungry dogs ready to lap up their blood on the field of conflict. This was no time for a trial prayer. This was no time to get out someone's book and try to find out how to pray.

It is too late to learn how to pray when the devil is breathing down your neck.

I do not find it recorded anywhere that Jephthah bowed down, tilted his head over, and folded his hands like an old diver getting ready to plunge into the pool. Jephthah is standing in the battlefield of mortal conflict, his very life at stake; and he cannot wait indefinitely for God to answer this prayer.

He needs to immediately touch the heart of God with prayer that will move His hand and bring an answer.

Hold On!

There is a woman in our congregation with the same determination as Jephthah. For twelve lonely years she suffered the anguish of separation from her husband because he spent everything he earned to buy drugs to snort up his nose. His drug habit cost several hundreds of dollars each and every day.

The man left his home and family, and he was gone for twelve years. Week after week his precious wife stood in the middle of our church and declared, "I believe I received when I prayed. My husband's coming home. I am not bowing my knee to the spirit of divorce. God can do all things. With man it is impossible, but with God all things are possible to him that believeth."

She said, "I am not letting go, I am holding on."

Her friends said, "Give up. He is a drug addict. Give up; he has left home for good. Give up."

"I cannot help it," she replied. "I believe I received when I prayed. I have already set my prayer in motion. God's already heard my prayer."

Now, the answer to that woman's prayer did not happen that afternoon, or that week.

It did not happen the first year, or the fifth year, or the tenth year.

Twelve long, lonely years later.

Was it worth the wait?

Yes! Absolutely!

Every time I see them, they are holding hands. God has put their lives and family back together because the husband finally yielded his will to the will of God!

Get the leaven out. We do not have to bow our knee to the spirit of divorce! God can keep a home together. The same God who parted the Red Sea can hold your home together.

What God does for others He will do for you, because God is no respecter of persons.

Do not quit — with God all things are possible.

Mix Your Praying With Your Giving

Prayer moves mountains.

It makes the low place high, and brings the high place low. Prayer makes the crooked way straight, and gives us hope when there is no hope. Prayer brings God on the scene — not a facsimile — but the real God who rides the wings of the morning.

Jephthah did not go home and put on his $1,000 suit and his lizard shoes. He did not outfit his wife in a designer dress or put bonnets on the kids' heads and say, "It's now 10:00 a.m; let's make sure we're out of there by noon."

Hannah, another Old Testament character, needed to reach God with her petition for a child, even though she was barren.

The Lord had shut up her womb (1 Samuel 1:5).

Hannah prayed, and vowed to give the child to the Lord if He would hear her cry.

And she vowed a vow, and said, O Lord of hosts, if thou wilt indeed look on the affliction of thine handmaid, and remember me, and not forget thine handmaid, but wilt give unto thine handmaid a man child, then I will give him unto the Lord all the days of his life and there shall no rasor come upon his head (v.11).

231

Many probably laughed and told her that her prayer to have a child was foolish. They said God would never answer a prayer like hers.

After all, God did not hear their prayers.

But, when Hannah prayed, it touched the heart of God. The answer invaded her body, and opened her once-barren womb.

> *Wherefore it came to pass, when the time was come about after Hannah had conceived, that she bare a son, and called his name Samuel, saying, Because I have asked him of the Lord (1 Samuel 1:20).*

God answered her prayers so abundantly that Hannah had many children.

> *And the Lord visited Hannah, so that she conceived, and bare three sons and two daughters (1 Samuel 2:21).*

And now, here is Jephthah, in the heat of battle, raising up his voice with the same intensity as Hannah:

> *And Jephthah vowed a vow unto the Lord, and said, If thou shalt without fail deliver the children of Ammon into mine hands,*
>
> *Then it shall be, that whatsoever cometh forth of the doors of my house to meet me, when I return in peace from the children of Ammon, shall surely be the Lord's, and I will offer it up for a burnt offering (Judges 11:30-31).*

Jephthah did the same thing Hannah did, and vowed his daughter to virginity in service to the Lord.

Jephthah and Hannah did the same thing Cornelius did. They all mixed their praying with their giving.

There was a certain man in Caesarea called Cornelius, a centurion of the band called the Italian band, a devout man, and one that feared God with all his house, which gave much alms to the people, and prayed to God alway. He saw in a vision evidently about the ninth hour of the day an angel of God coming in to him, and saying unto him, Cornelius. And when he looked on him, he was afraid, and said, What is it, Lord? And he said unto him, Thy prayers and thine alms are come up for a memorial before God (Acts 10:1-4).

Cornelius prayed, and offered alms as a memorial to his God.

Hannah and Jephthah also mixed their praying with their giving. Jephthah said, "God, if you will deliver this enemy into my hands, if you will deliver the children of Ammon into my hand, and I return home in peace, then whatever comes out of my house to greet me I will give it to you."

Understand the depth of this giving. Jephthah did not say, "I will go inside, find some trinket, and bring it out and offer it to you." He said, "Anything that comes out, God, belongs to you."

Here was a desperate man. Here was a man crying out to God, and he needed his prayer answered NOW. He didn't fumble through his prayer journal. He didn't get out the latest book on microwave miracles through prayer.

No!

He reached down deep within himself. He knew prayer mixed with giving immediately gets God's attention ... because giving is an act of faith.

The Lord delivered Ammon into his hands. Jephthah did not wait six months for an answer. Over 40,000 men were slaughtered that day at the sword of Jephthah, who moments before faced utter defeat.

He had learned to mix his prayer with sacrificial giving.

If we are to get the leaven out as we approach the end of this age, we must learn to do the same — mix our praying with sacrificial giving that reflects the intensity of our heart to follow Him.

In the midst of his imprisonment in the sewer systems of Rome, Paul lifted up his voice and exclaimed, "God has highly exalted me and given me joint seating together with Christ in heavenly places."

Today, we are involved in the greatest revolution that has ever transpired in the history of the Church, and I believe God is going to use men and women who have had enough of Gospel rhetoric and slick-haired, shiny-shoed evangelists.

We have had enough of the doctrines of men.

It is time someone gave us a word from the Lord.

It is time someone stood on the platforms of America and exclaimed, "Thus saith the Word of the living God."

It is time for revival.

The Devil's Map

Let me illustrate where I believe the Church is and where it has the opportunity of going.

Many men have tried to conquer the world, but few have ever even come close to attaining that goal.

Alexander the Great, at seventeen years of age, sat down on the portico steps of the great coliseum in Rome, put his head in his hands, and began to weep. His generals rushed to his side and asked, "Why do you weep, Alexander?"

"There are no more worlds left to conquer," he sobbed.

Hitler tried. He committed heinous crimes, leading six million Jews to the gas chambers, and wrought havoc on the entire planet.

Another man came very close. His name was Napoleon. It is said that he would gather his warlords together and would spread out a map of the world. As they reviewed the map, suddenly his finger would raise in the air and plunge into the center of that map, always landing on a little red spot out in the middle of the ocean — a little place called England.

As his finger landed on that red spot, his face would

235

cringe, and his voice would heighten until his warlords trembled. He would roar, "Were it not for that red spot, I could conquer the world!"

On a lonely hillside outside of Jerusalem a carpenter hung between heaven and earth. And there, the scorching Palestinian sun beat down into His open wounds until it felt as though the very flames of hell had embedded themselves in the flesh of the only begotten Son of God.

I believe as He hung between heaven and earth, from the darkened regions of the demonic underworld, Satan raised his crooked finger ... and with a heinous scowl upon his face, he pointed toward Golgotha's hillside and screamed, "Were it not for that red spot, I could conquer the world."

There's a red spot on the face of the earth today, and the howling hordes of the demonic realm, swirling in the upper atmosphere, are cringing and shaking. They are calling in their legions and refortifying their fortresses.

They are pointing to a remnant of the New Testament Church that is bold enough and brave enough to proclaim, "We're going to preach the old-fashioned, Holy Ghost Gospel of Jesus Christ, whether the devil likes it or not!"

There's much to be gained from a return to the discarded values of the past. Thank God for preachers that will tell you that hell is hot and eternity is long. Thank God for men that are not just puppets, but men that will get behind the sacred pulpit of God and begin to cry out like prophets.

I believe the John the Baptists of our generation are coming out of the wilderness crying loud and sparing not.

In 1815, Napoleon rolled out his map again before the Battle of Waterloo, and with his finger traced the jagged edge of a great nation. He said, "Gentlemen, here lies a sleeping giant. If it ever recognizes its mineral wealth and ties it to its manpower, let the world bow its knee to it and tremble." He outlined the nation of China, saying, "It's a sleeping giant. Shhh, let it sleep. Let it sleep. Don't arouse it from its slumber."

In like manner, Satan is reviewing the map of the ages, and as he does, the corridors of hell ring with the words, "Let them wallow in the leaven of religiosity. Let them have their church socials, their committees, and all their plans and programs. Let them come to church and go home soothing their consciences. But if they ever wake up and understand the power of the blood and the authority of the name of Jesus, we will tremble before this sleeping giant they call the Church.

It is Time to Cry Out

Cry aloud, spare not, lift up thy voice like a trumpet, and shew my people their transgression (Isaiah 58:1).

The Bible does not say "whisper." The Bible does not say "Be real nice, and real soft, and real quiet and try to be everyone's friend."

The Bible does not say, "Try to fit in with the religious crowd, and don't ruffle their feathers."

The Bible says, "It is time for us not to be ashamed to CRY LOUD, not to be ashamed to SPARE NOT, to lift up our voice like a trumpet and show the people their transgressions.

> *Cry aloud, spare not, lift up thy voice like a trumpet, and shew my people their transgression, and the house of Jacob their sins (Isaiah 58:1).*

It is time for change in the Church.

God has a remnant on this planet who knows His name, a remnant who will stand up and declare, "It is time for the prophetic unction and voice of God to ring from the highest housetops. It is time to tell men there is only one way to heaven, and His name is Jesus."

John declares,

> *Verily, verily, I say unto you, If a man keep my saying, he shall never see death (John 8:51).*

Remember, that word *keep* means "to chaperon, like a father would his virgin daughter."

There is a group of people who want to KEEP, who want to protect the Gospel. They are manning their battle stations. They have heard the war cry of the great God Jehovah, and they are coming out of the cracks and crevices and out of holes they have dug in fear. They have heard the trumpeting voice of God exclaim, "If I am for you, do not fear what men can do to you. For what can man do unto you if I am for you? No man can be against you. And greater is He that is in you than he that is in the world."

There is only one reason why Communism fell in the former Soviet Union.

There is only one reason they now totter on the brink of economic ruin and famine.

That reason is idolatry.

They raised mere mortals to the status of gods. Look in God's Word. When idolatry is practiced in a nation, agricultural ruin follows. God withholds rain, sends plagues and hail and other freaks of nature.

I was in Russia the week after the failed coup, and I witnessed the fall of the great Communist institutions. While preaching one of the first Gospel rallies in Russia in over seventy years, I raised my Bible and said, "This is a Bible. It tells of God's love and man's fall. Lenin came and went. Stalin came and went. Mussolini came and went, but God's Word is eternal."

The Word of God has withstood the deadening blows of the haters of God throughout the ages, and it will withstand them today in this final hour.

I do not care what the world tries to do to the Gospel truth; they cannot stop it. They can try to bury it, but it will resurrect itself and beat the pallbearers back to the house.

This Word's going to stand against the world.

It is time for a renaissance revival of the basic Bible elements of truth that once made this nation great!

239

If we are going to get the leaven out of the Church, we are going to have to return to the basic tenents of the Bible. I know that in this philosophical age of theological mishmash, everyone has some new revelation, but I am not looking for new revelation. The greatest revelation from the Bible I have ever received is found in John 3:16:

> *For God so loved the world, that he gave his only begotten Son, that whosoever believeth in him should not perish, but have everlasting life.*

Jesus Will Bring Us Out!

It is time to proclaim that a resurrected Savior shed His blood for lost humanity.

He is the only one who can get the leaven out of the Church today.

> *And God spake all these words, saying, I am the Lord thy God, which have brought thee out of the land of Egypt, out of the house of bondage (Exodus 20:1,2).*

He brought us out of the miry clay.

> *He brought me up also out of an horrible pit, out of the miry clay, and set my feet upon a rock, and established my goings (Psalm 40:2).*

Forty-four times in the first five books of the Bible, God reminds the children of Israel, "I am the God that brought you out!"

There is only one way to get the leaven out of the Church.

The God we serve is still a saving Jesus. He is still a healing Jesus. He is still a delivering Jesus.

Only He can take the leaven out.

In one moment, in one prayer, without the aid of any organization, He took an alcoholic of thirty-five years and cleaned him up, straightened him up and sobered him up .... so that five years later he is still sitting on the edge of the third pew with his hands raised without ever again touching one drop of alcohol.

He took a $500 a day crack user, cleaned him up and put him in the church choir.

He can lead people out of the homeless shelters and into salvation.

This is the God we serve.

It is time someone started telling the truth about Jesus. He can change lives.

He can get the leaven out.

When my wife and I were newlyweds, I received a bill for one of my credit cards with notations that read: "Bright White Cleaners, World Harvest Church, Bob's Gasoline, Mellons, World Harvest Church, Mellons, Good Gospel Bookstore, Mellons."

I called my wife and said, "Darling, you have been cooking some wonderful meals, but I do not remember ever eating any melons, yet they are all over this bank card statement."

241

She said, "Why Honey, *Mellons* is the name of my favorite dress shop!"

As I hung up the phone, I suddenly realized my wife was not taking my name in vain, but she was making full use of my name!

It's time to stop taking the name of Jesus in vain, and start making FULL USE of it!

The first use of that name is found in Matthew.

And she shall bring forth a son, and thou shalt call his name Jesus: for he shall save his people from their sins (Matthew 1:21).

Many have renounced the provision of the name of Jesus.

We do not know what salvation is anymore. We think it is walking down an aisle, or signing a piece of paper, or going to church.

We will never get to heaven by going to church, or by being a nice person. We will never get to heaven paying taxes, or by being involved in the community.

We can never earn salvation — it is the gift of God's divine grace!

There is only one way to heaven — Jesus.

There is only One who can get the leaven of sin out of our lives — Jesus.

Jesus said, "I am the way, I am the truth and I am the light."

Nicodemus, a Pharisee, came to Jesus and said, "How can I have what you have?"

Jesus responded,

Verily, verily, I say unto thee, Except a man be born again, he cannot see the kingdom of God (John 3:3).

Jesus said we must be born-again. Anyone teaching anything else is a false prophet and must be ignored.

Nicodemus asked,

How can a man be born when he is old? can he enter the second time into his mother's womb, and be born? (John 3:4).

Jesus answered,

Verily, verily, I say unto thee, Except a man be born of water and of the Spirit, he cannot enter into the kingdom of God (John 3:5).

All of us are partakers of flesh and blood; we are in an earth suit. Just look down at what is dangling from the ends of our arms — hands and fingers. Inside our chest, a heart is beating and lungs are expanding. Blood is flowing through our veins. We are in an earth suit, eating natural food to sustain natural life.

We have absolutely no problem believing we are flesh and blood.

Forasmuch then as the children are partakers of flesh and blood, he also himself likewise took part of the same; that through death he might destroy him that had the power of death, that is, the devil (Hebrews 2:14).

243

Death Conquered

The last obstacle to be conquered was death.

At a funeral not long ago, I stood by the casket of a dear saint of God who was eighty-eight years old. She laid there in that casket, and when her family walked by, I told them, "Now, take a good long look and get it embedded in your heart. This is a Christian. It is an odd species. We do not find many of them anymore. This is a real Christian."

If she could talk to us, she would say, "Do not weep for me. I am in a country where there aren't any wheelchairs or funeral homes or morticians or drug wars. There aren't any babies with swollen bellies or mommies with breasts dried up because they cannot get enough food to sustain natural life. There aren't any babies born in hovels with rats gnawing on their toes and fingers."

We are on our way to a city whose builder and maker is God, and we are not defeated.

Every foe is vanquished, all leaven has been cleansed — because Christ is Lord indeed.

I have been baptized not in vinegar, but in victory! My entire being is inundated with the glory of God. I am convinced that greater is He that is in me than he that is in this sin-sick, hell-bound world!

He is bigger than our flesh, bigger than this planet! Jesus said, "He that believeth in Me, though he were dead, yet shall he live!"

Think about it.

There is no foe bigger than death. Death is the captain sitting on the throne of every adversity, every plague, every torment in the life of humanity.

Leaven is slow, certain death. But through God and the power of His Son, Jesus, who ascended on that heavenly throne, death has been grabbed by the nape of the neck and cast off. Jesus has declared, "I am Alpha. I am Omega. I was dead, but I am alive forevermore."

Jesus transcends the natural world.

He transcends the polluting, corrosive effects of leaven.

We are in touch with an eternal God who lives within us!

He rides the wild wings of the morning!

He is the Lord of glory!

And, if He is God, then let us serve Him.

Let us crown him King of Kings and Lord of Lords!

With all our heart, mind, soul and strength, let us serve Him.

My heart is free. I have no fear of the past, the present or the future. For what shall men do unto me? If God is for me, who can be against me?

The demon hordes of hell are under our feet. Our bodies are full of the healing power of God. We have victory from the top of our heads to the soles of our feet. God is making a way for us where there is no way. God is making our feet like hinds' feet. He slips His everlasting arms under us and keeps us from falling. He bears us up on angels wings.

245

Bring Back the Emotion

Someone said, "Well, I just do not believe in all this emotionalism."

If we received an unexpected thousand dollar bill, we would believe in emotionalism.

So why not get emotional about Jesus? He owns the cattle on a thousand hills.

Some people say, "Well now, Brother Rod, some people worship that way, some people get excited, but not us. We are different."

It only holds true so far that everyone reacts differently. I guarantee that if I put a paper clip in the hands of one hundred people and let each of them stick that clip in a light socket, every one of them would have the same reaction.

We have something the power company does not even know about. We have been endued with power from on high!

He also himself likewise took part of the same; that through death He might destroy him that had the power of death, that is, the devil; and deliver them who through fear of death were all their lifetime subject to bondage (Hebrews 2:14,15).

Jesus destroyed the power of death!

Three Deaths Defeated

There are three kinds of death: physical death, spiritual death, and what the book of Revelation calls "the second death."

Let us look at physical death first.

One of these days, unless Jesus comes for the rapture of the Church first, they are going to take this body of mine and fold my hands over the top of my chest and lay me down in a casket. A few people may say, "Well, we will miss him."

If I could, I would wink at them.

Don't be dripping tears on this body, because my Jesus went to an old hill outside Jerusalem called Calvary, and He shed His life's blood for me. He hung His head and gave up the ghost. Close by that scene we find the borrowed tomb of Joseph of Arimathaea. It is not significant because of who is there; it is significant because of who is not there. On the third day a great angel said, "Mary, go and tell them that the Son of God is risen."

Jesus is alive and well.

When He conquered death, He gave us the power to conquer all leaven and the death it brings.

When Jesus rose from the dead, He said, "I pried the keys of death and hell out of the unyielding hands of the Antichrist. I locked them to my girdle. I rode out of the harrowing halls of the devil's perdition and into heaven."

If tomorrow death finds me missing, the Bible will tell you where I am. It declares that to be absent from the body is to be present with the Lord.

We can live not afraid to die. We can wink at death's angel and say, "Transport me into the pavilions of glory prepared for me from the foundation of time."

Unleavened, Eternal life

We can have all the leaven of the world, all the money any man could have, all the business prowess any man could have, all the respect of this world, all the pleasures of this world, but one day we will be staring death in the face and our eyes are going to close for the very last time.

One of these days we are going to lace our shoes for the very last time, kiss our spouse goodbye for the very last time, get in the car and drive to the office for the very last time.

Many in this world throw up their hands and cry, "I do not know what is coming after that."

Do you want to know what makes us emotional?

What makes us run?

We know what is coming after death!

You could take out a gun, pull back the hammer, put your hand around that steel-handled weapon, put your finger on the trigger and pull it back.

Pow!

That bullet could strike me with the force of death, and instantly kill me.

But do not weep for me!

Do not cry or sorrow for me.

You might make my body fall down, but you cannot kill me.

I am alive forever! I am no longer subject to bondage through fear of physical death.

I know a young preacher who was at the bedside of a saint of God about to change her eternal address. He looked at her as he stroked her silvery hair with his hand and said, "Mama, aren't you just a little bit afraid?"

She replied, "Son, I am not afraid. This old Book here by my bedside tells me that my Father owns the land on both sides of the river."

The Bible declares that the foundations of that heavenly city are not made of concrete and steel, but of the very finest precious jewels: jasper, emerald, topaz, sardius and amethyst.

God poured jewels into the foundation.

Honestly, it really would not matter to me if the gates of heaven were made of wood or if they swung on leather hinges. It would not matter to me if there was mud in the streets knee-deep, and the mansions were nothing more than cardboard shanties. Because, when I look down the end of that muddy street, at the end of that heavenly boulevard, I will see the One who took my place.

When I deserved death, He cancelled my debt.

249

When I deserved eternity in the bowels of hell, He sealed my pardon and marked my bill "Paid in Full."

He tasted death, so that we, who through the fear of death were subject to bondage, might be free.

That he by the grace of God should taste death for every man ... and deliver them who through fear of death were all their lifetime subject to bondage (Heb 2:9,15).

Job said this life is but a vapor; it is seen and it is gone. Man's life is short and full of trouble. But I am going to a city where shoes do not ever need polishing, and suits do not ever need pressing.

I have an investment on the other side.

I have a grandmama who was one of the greatest Christians I ever knew there waiting for me. How my heart misses her. How I wish I could just pick up the phone and talk to her.

I did not need the leaven of religion, I needed a Savior.

I was dying and on my way to hell, and He gave me hope.

Sitting on the ash heap, his body full of boils, his children dead, his business bankrupt, his barns burned, and his wife begging him to curse God and die, Job said, I cannot do it, for I know my Redeemer lives *(Job 19:25).*

Get the leaven out!

The Rising Dead

Tell the drug lords and the New Age philosophers about eternal life and Jesus. Tell them to stop looking for reincarnation. We can get off this planet. We can be catapulted extraterrestrial into the presence of God. When we lay this fleshly body down, we will exchange it for an immortal body in the presence of God forever."

"Well, Brother Rod, we shouldn't talk about heaven. I mean, there is a lot of work to do on this earth."

Yes there is, but my Bible also says,

Behold, I shew you a mystery; we shall not all sleep, but we shall all be changed, in a moment, in the twinkling of an eye, at the last trump: for the trumpet shall sound, and the dead shall be raised incorruptible, and we shall be changed (1 Corinthians 15:51,52).

The dead in Christ are going to rise first, then we which are alive and remain are going to be caught up into the clouds to be with the Lord, and so shall we ever be with the Lord. The passage ends with this statement:

Therefore, my beloved brethren, be ye stedfast, unmoveable, always abounding in the work of the Lord, forasmuch as ye know that your labour is not in vain in the Lord (v.58).

Don't tell me I cannot talk about heaven!

If all we need is a self-help program, we can get that from the world.

251

If all we need is a business seminar, we can get that from the world.

There is nothing wrong with those things, but God intended more for His people.

The Bible gives us a reason for living when dying looks easy. And it lets us know not only how to live, but how to die.

We can cleanse the leaven from our lives.

We have defeated cancer, arthritis and the common cold. We have gone beyond that, and through Jesus, we have defeated death itself!

We are here because one day we are going to die, we are going to experience the separation of the spirit and soul from the earth suit in which we have lived. Through the cross of Christ and the blood that splashed on the dusty sand of Calvary that day, the bondage of death has been broken.

In ancient Rome, a criminal who was found guilty of the crime of first degree murder was forced to walk the streets with the body of the one he had murdered strapped to his own back. Finally, the decay of that body of death would infect the murderer's own body until he died also.

Paul said, "That is the way I was. I was walking around with a body of death on me and I could not get it off. And I cried out, 'Who shall deliver me from this body of death? Who can take it off me?'"

O wretched man that I am! who shall deliver
me from the body of this death? (Romans 7:24).

I thank God that the law of life in Christ Jesus has freed me from the law of sin and death.

For the law of the Spirit of life in Christ
Jesus hath made me free from the law of sin
and death (Romans 8:2).

When death's chilly fingers wrap their stranglehold around our bodies, we will not fear.

Yea, thou I walk through the valley of the
shadow of death, I will fear no evil: for thou
art with me (Psalm 23:4).

Spiritual Death

Man was created to fellowship with God. In Genesis 3, sin formed a barrier between the Creator and the created. Without repentance and the acceptance of Jesus as Savior with His blood as the propitiation for our sin ... man abides in a perpetual state of spiritual death.

We are in the last days. This is it. This is the grand finale. We are in the locker room for the pre-game briefing of the super bowl of the ages being played out on this planet between the forces of darkness and the forces of light.

Our Commander in Chief is standing just as a coach in the locker room before the big game, and He is saying: "I have some strategies for you. They are going to shoot the gap. Don't worry about it; we are going to double team them. No, I'll tell you what we'll do; we'll triple team them. The Father, the Son and the Holy Ghost will block in front of us!"

When this planet is rocking and reeling like a drunken man; when the seas are seething, and the moon is bleeding, and the world is dying — the Bible will remain the only constant source of life and blessing. It is the inerrant, infallible, unadulterated, pure Word of the living God.

Rely on it in life or in death; it has the answers.

But there is leaven because we are carnal Christians. It is in our minds, our motives and our ministries.

We have to crucify it.

The Bible will deliver us from the fear and bondage of carnality and its death. Only through the Word can we be free from the leaven Paul describes: backbiting, envy, strife, revelling, heresy, sedition, lust and murder.

Paul could write the same message today to the church in Columbus, or Miami, or Orlando, or Los Angeles, or Dallas, or Tallahassee or Fort Lauderdale.

To be carnal minded is death.

How do I get rid of that body of death?

How did Christ overcome it?

He gave us his Word, and we have victory over the death of the carnal mind.

Let this mind be in you which was in Christ Jesus also (Phillipians 2:5).

The Second Death

The third arena of death for which the cross of Christ secured our liberty is the second death.

God gave us absolute dominion over death.

Why do we spend so much of our time on the peripheral edges of Christian experience, preaching and teaching, having seminars and week-long conventions on the trivialities of Gospel truth.

If death is conquered, everything else is elementary.

What is sickness? Limited death. If death has already been defeated, then sickness is defeated.

And I saw an angel come down from heaven, having the key of the bottomless pit and a great chain in his hand.

And he laid hold on the dragon, that old serpent, which is the Devil, and Satan, and bound him a thousand years.

And cast him into the bottomless pit, and shut him up, and set a seal upon him, that he should not deceive the nations no more, till the thousand years should be fulfilled: and after that he must be loosed a little season.

And I saw thrones, and they that sat upon them, and judgment was given unto them: and I saw the souls of them that were beheaded for the witness of Jesus, and for the word of God, and which had not worshipped the beast, neither his image, neither had received his mark upon their foreheads, or in their hands; and they lived and reigned with Christ a thousand years (Revelation 20:1-4).

255

At this time, the rapture of the Church spoken of in 1 Thessalonians has transpired, and the Church of Jesus Christ has been around the throne of God for seven years, celebrating in the marriage supper of the Lamb.

During that time the world will have experienced seven years of the most horrendous tribulation ever to hit the earth. Jesus himself said,

For then shall be great tribulation, such as was not since the beginning of the world to this time, no, nor ever shall be (Matthew 24:21).

The last day of the tribulation period becomes the first day of the millennial reign of Christ ... suddenly, God will give the decree.

The heavenly chariots that haven't ridden the wind since Elijah will be pulled from their stalls. Jesus Christ, himself, will arise from the marriage supper table. He'll slide his long, lean Gallilean leg over a great white stallion, and the crack of his whip will billow out with the crash of a thousand cannons.

The Bible says He's coming back to this earth, and all his saints will be with Him. We are going to be riding with Him when He returns to this planet.

Talk about victory over death!

He's coming back. He's not coming wrapped in swaddling clothes and laid in a manger, or as an effeminate looking, long-haired, sandal-shoed, flowing-gowned person walking around the Sea of Galilee.

I saw heaven opened, and behold a white horse; and he that sat upon him was called Faithful and True, and in righteousness he doth judge and make war.

His eyes were as a flame of fire, and on his head were many crowns; and he had a name written, that no man new, but he himself.

And he was clothed with a vesture dipped in blood: and his name is called The Word of God.

And the armies which were in heaven followed him upon white horses, clothed in fine linen, white and clean.

And out of his mouth goeth a sharp sword, that with it he should smite the nations: and He shall rule them with a rod of iron: and he treadeth the winepress of the fierceness and wrath of Almighty God.

And he hath on his vesture and on his thigh a name written, KING OF KINGS, AND LORD OF LORDS (Revelation 19:11-16).

Let the kings of the earth tremble, and the demon hordes quake in horror. The King of Glory shall come through!

He has crushed the tormenting, demonic powers that have ruled this planet since Genesis chapter three.

He has gathered his saints unto Himself from the four winds of the earth. They will be with him when He comes back to defeat the Antichrist and his army in the Valley of Meggido.

Without lifting His sword, He'll look across the Valley of Meggido and speak one word. The Bible says, their flesh will consume away while they stand upon their feet, and their eyes shall consume away in their holes, and their tongue shall consume away in their mouth *(Zechariah 14:12)*.

He is coming down through the Kidron Valley, through the eastern gate to Temple Mount where He will rule and reign for a thousand years of peace. At the end of that time will come the judgment.

> *And I saw a great white throne, and him that sat on it, from whose face the earth and the heaven fled away; and there was found no place for them.*
>
> *And I saw the dead, small and great, stand before God; and the books were opened: and another book was opened, which is the book of life: and the dead were judged out of those things which were written in the books, according to the works.*
>
> *And the sea gave up the dead which were in it; and death and hell delivered up the dead which were in them: and they were judged every man according to their works.*
>
> *And death and hell were cast into the lake of fire. This is the second death.*

And whosoever was not found written in
the book of life was cast into the lake of fire
(Revelation 20:11-15).

We, who through the fear of death were all our life-time subject to bondage have been freed — freed from physical death, freed from spiritual death, freed from carnality, freed from the second death.

...that through death he took part of the
same; that through death he might destroy him
that had the power of death, that is the devil; And
deliver them, who through fear of death were all
their lifetime subject to bondage (Hebrews
2:14,15).

If you go to hell, you will be an intruder upon Satan and his hordes for all eternity. Hell was not made for you!

The Choice of Leavened or Unleavened

The choice we have today is God or the devil, heaven or hell, life or death, blessing or cursing, leavened or unleavened.

That is it.

If we choose Christ, then hell and death, cursing, and leaven have no power on us.

But if we reject Him, we will stand at the Great White Throne of Judgment looking at a gaping, unbearable blankness in the Book of Life. We will say in our heart, "There it is. There is the place where my name

259

should have been, where Jesus Christ the Son of God stood poised and ready to record my name ... but I said 'no'."

In this endtime hour of spiritual history, it is time to shun the shallow flatlands of spiritual mediocrity and to go all the way with Jesus.

It is time to cleanse our hearts of leaven.

Examine your heart.

If it is cold or indifferent toward God, if you are not on fire, not excited about the things of God, if you do not feel the life and power of God in every part and portion of your being ... then get the leaven out and get right with God!

God, deliver us from the leaven of death and make us eternally alive!

Follow the Unleavened Leaders

The way to a life free of leaven is through the simple, plain, unadulterated Gospel.

God created man, but man committed sin and high treason against God and fell in the Garden of Eden. At that moment, God began to build a bridge — a bridge that would bring men and women back to a place of fellowship with Him.

Cross over the Gospel bridge, restored and purified of leaven, and cry out to God:

Lord, let your holy anointing rest upon us like a mantle.

Let the anointing that destroys every yoke come upon us.

Let us wear it like a garment.

Let your supernatural power flow from our bellies.

Let your healing power shoot from our hands like lightening from a thunder storm.

May we raise up a remnant Church that will be a light to the entire world, and may every stronghold of Satan tremble as we get up each morning.

May those frozen by the icy grip of religious tradition begin to thaw under your prophetic voice.

Where Are Our Leaders?

I was sitting in a restaurant not long ago when the Spirit of God came upon me, and I began to weep. The restaurant was crowded with people, yet I was weeping.

My wife asked me what was the matter; and looking up through those tears, I said, "Where have all our leaders gone?"

There has been an absence, a quiet abyss of blackness and darkness surrounding the body of Christ. We know that troubled times drive men of God to prayer and into His presence ... but is that happening today?

We need more leaders willing to seek God!

Where Are Our Prophets?

Even in Biblical times, there came a lull in the prophetic voices of the nation of Israel. The children of Israel could only find Dr. Sounding Brass and Dr. Dumbbell, trying to dissuade them from the realities of the Word of God.

And so it is with us today.

The thundering voice of the prophets seems to have been silenced. We have almost lost sight of old-fashioned, Holy Ghost inspired preaching.

For too long, the Church has been out of balance in the ministry gifts. There have been an abundance of teachers in the ministry, but not enough of the rest of the fivefold ministry gifts in the body of Christ. Teachers are vitally important, but God intended for all the ministry gifts to be manifested in His New Testament Church, not just the ministry of teachers.

And he gave some, apostles; and some, prophets; and some, evangelists; and some, pastors and teachers;

For the perfecting of the saints, for the work of the ministry, for the edifying of the body of Christ:

Till we all come in the unity of the faith, and of the knowledge of the Son of God, unto a perfect man, unto the measure of the stature of the fulness of Christ (Ephesians 4:11-13).

Without the Church functioning in the full power of the fivefold ministry, the lost have been plummeting over the chasm into eternal hell faster than the unlocked wheels of time can carry them.

There seems to be no one to reach one hand into

glory and the other into the gutter to rescue depraved, dying, desperate humanity from the abyss of the satanic underworld called hell.

But I have good news today ... those men of God did not vanish from the earth!

They have been revived and refueled.

The Church is waking up!

We are more determined.

We are bolder.

We are holding up the blood-stained banner of the cross of Christ, and trampling the devil under our feet, pursuing, overtaking and recovering all that Satan has stolen from us.

The Church is ready to cleanse and purify itself of leaven.

Popularity Versus Truth

Sin, and the wages of sin, is not a popular message. But the Bible declares,

And they that shall be of thee shall build the old waste places: thou shalt raise up the foundations of many generations; and thou shalt be called, The repairer of the breach, The restorer of paths to dwell in (Isaiah 58:12).

Stop trying to get across the bridge through religiosity. Stop trying to go through life full of the leaven of the Galatians.

Get in touch with the supernatural workings of God.

Be baptized in the Holy Ghost.

Break the bonds of sin.

Stop trying to work your way to heaven, and accept the freely-given grace of Christ as your Savior.

Judgment stares us all in the face.

The road of life inevitably ends up at the crossroads of the cross.

No one can bypass it.

On the blood-stained cross of Christ, one hand points toward heaven and the other towards hell, Jesus asks,

"Heaven or hell?

Life or death?

Blessing or cursing?

Unleavened or leavened?"

Choose, but choose at the cross.

God has shown us how to make the old Gospel bridge right.

Get the leaven out!

This is the message Satan did not want the world to hear!

God has absolutely nothing more to give us!

If we are looking for God to give us something else, we are looking amiss. He already gave us everything He had when He gave us Jesus. Calvary is a completed work.

God has nothing left to give — no healing, no deliverance. He has already given Himself; and when we receive Him, we receive the answer to every prayer we will ever pray.

We do not need healing, we just need Jesus — for

He is the Healer. He is the Deliverer. He is the Victor. He is joy, and the answer to every need of our lives. Where He is, darkness disappears. Where He is, the power of sorrow is broken. Welcome His presence! Enjoy His presence! Practice being in His presence. He is Creator, Deliverer, Healer, Majesty, Might, Power and Dominion.

But God cannot bless us beyond our last act of disobedience — beyond our last taste of leavened bread.

If you are not a tither, get rid of the leaven that puts the love of money before God. Do not give in to fear! Start giving ten percent of your income into the body of Christ today.

Repent.

Ask God to forgive you for robbing Him, and He will forgive you as you determine to change.

Many of us are like the prodigal son. We want the Father's possessions, but we do not want the Father's presence.

We want what He has, but we do not want Him.

This strong word may be the very key to unlock the womb of the Church to reach the lost.

So many people are confused about the last book of the Bible, but there is no reason to be confused about it. In fact, if there was any generation in the history of the world that should understand the book of Revelation, it is this one.

God wrote it for us.

We are watching prophecy being fulfilled every day.

Thank God for it. We have a marvelous road map called the Bible. All we need to do is read it and follow it.

We don't need the evening news. Just read the Bible, and you will know the news before it happens.

What a Book!

What a victory!

What a triumph!

God's Word!

When we find the Bible, we find life.

When we find the Bible, we find victory and power.

I pray the heretics will see the light.

I pray the false prophets will come to know God.

I pray the religious dead will find life in Christ.

But if they never do they still cannot stop revival.

They cannot stop the outpouring of the Holy Ghost.

They cannot stop the signs and wonders that are destined for this generation.

They cannot stop us from getting ALL the leaven out of our lives once and for all.

Nothing can stop us.

The greatest revival we have ever seen, heard of, or read about has begun.

God help us to awake, assume our positions, and move out in your power.

Help us to fulfill our purpose as the final remnant of the New Testament Church ... to usher in the great endtime harvest and the triumphant return of our Lord Jesus Christ!

And the spirit and the bride say, come. And let him that heareth say, Come. And let him that is athirst come. And whosoever will, let him take the water of life freely ... He which testifieth these things saith, Surely I come quickly. Amen. even so, come, Lord Jesus (Revelation 22:17,20).

FOOTNOTES

INTRODUCTION
SPIRITUAL AIDS RAVISHES THE UNSUSPECTING CHURCH

1. Day, Lorraine, M.D., "A Killer Among Us." *Religious Broadcasting*, February 1993, 24.

2. Ibid, 25.

3. Ibid.

4. Ibid.

5. Harris, R. Laird, Gleason L. Archer, Jr., and Bruce K. Waltke, *Theological Wordbook of the Old Testament 2.* Chicago: Moody Press, 1980, 939.

6. "False Premises: The Assumptions that Hinder Ministry." *Ministry Currents 2*, No. 4, October-December 1992, 2-4.

7. Ibid, 3.

8. Dante, Alighieri, *The Divine Comedy*. New York, New York: W.W. Norton & Co., 1961.

9. *Religion Report 7*, No. 7, March 1993, 8.

CHAPTER ONE
THE CORROSIVE EFFECTS OF LEAVEN

1. Hoffman, Mark S., ed. *The World Almanac and Book of Facts*. New York, New York: Pharos Books, 1992, 947.

2. Gianakaris, C.J., *Plutarch*. New York, New York: Twayne Publishers, Inc., 1970.

3. Foxe, John, "Wendelmuta, A Widow." *Foxe's Book of Martyrs*, London: Adam & Company, 14, Ivy Lane, Paternoster Row, and Newcastle-Uper-Tyne, n.d., 159-160.

4. Ibid.

5. Ravenhill, Leonard, *Revival God's Way*. Minneapolis, Minnesota: Bethany House Publishers, 1986, 50.

CHAPTER THREE
THE LEAVEN OF THE SADDUCEES

1. Stamphill, Ira, "Mansion Over the Hilltop." Cited from *Melodies of Praise*, Springfield, Missouri: Gospel Publishing House, 1957, 45.

2. "The Generation That Forgot God: The Baby Boom Goes Back to Church and Church Will Never Be the Same." *Time*, 5 April 1993, 44-49.

3. Hoffman, *World Almanac*, 947.

CHAPTER FOUR
THE LEAVEN OF THE HERODIANS

1. Josephus, Flavius, *The Works of Josephus*. Translated by William Whiston, A.M., Peabody, Massachusetts: Hedrickson Publishers, 1987, 596.

2. *Columbus Dispatch*, 24 November 1990, 5D.

3. "The Hidden Cost of Aids." *U.S. News & World Report*, 27 July 1992, 58.

4. Lindsay, Gordon, *The John G. Lake Sermons on Dominion over Demons, Disease and Death*. Dallas, Texas: Christ For the Nations, 1978, 108.

CHAPTER FIVE
THE LEAVEN OF THE CORINTHIANS

1. Webster, Daniel, *Webster's Ninth New Collegiate Dictionary*. Springfield, Massachusetts: Merriam-Webster Inc., n.d., 290.

CHAPTER SIX
THE LEAVEN OF THE GALATIANS

1. Havner, Vance, *Truth for Each Day*. Westwood, New Jersey, 1962, 27.

2. Widmeyer, C.B., "Come and Dine." Cited from *Melodies of Praise*, Springfield, Missouri: Gospel Publishing House, 1957, 20.

3. Stamphill, "Mansion Over the Hill Top," 45.

4. Lowry, Robert, "Nothing but the Blood." Cited from *Melodies of Praise*, Springfield, Missouri: Gospel Publishing House, 1957, 270.

5. Knight, Walter B., *Walter B. Knight's 1001 Illustrations*. Grand Rapids, Michigan: Wm. B. Erdmann's Publishing Co., 1956, 851.

6. Spafford, Horatio G. and P.P. Bliss, "It Is Well With My Soul." Cited from *101 Hymn Stories*, Edited by Kenneth W. Osbeck, Grand Rapids, Michigan: Kregel Publications, 1982, 44.

7. Grape, John T., "Jesus Paid It All." Cited from *Melodies of Praise*, Springfield, Missouri: Gospel Publishing House, 1957, 127.

8. Hudson, R.E., "At the Cross." Cited from *Melodies of Praise*, Springfield, Missouri: Gospel Publishing House, 1957, 273.

9. Newton, John, "Amazing Grace." Cited from *Melodies of Praise*, Springfield, Missouri: Gospel Publishing House, 1957, 272.

10. Watts, Issac, "When the Battle's Over." Cited from *Melodies of Praise*, Springfield, Missouri: Gospel Publishing House, 1957, 148.

CHAPTER SEVEN
THE CLEANSING SOLUTION

1. Criswell, W.A., *These Issues We Must Face.* Grand Rapids, Michigan: Zondervan Publishing House, 1953, 46.

2. Ibid.

3. Bradbury, William B., "Sweet Hour of Prayer." Cited from *Melodies of Praise*, Springfield, Missouri: Gospel Publishing House, 1957, 304.

ABOUT THE AUTHOR ...

Rod Parsley began his ministry as an energetic 19-year-old, in the backyard of his parent's Ohio home. The fresh, "old-time gospel" approach of Parsley's delivery immediately attracted a hungry, God-seeking audience. From the 17 people who attended that first 1976 backyard meeting, the crowds grew rapidly.

Today, as the pastor of Columbus, Ohio's 5,200 seat World Harvest Church, Parsley oversees World Harvest's Preschool-12 Christian Academy; World Harvest Bible Institute; and numerous church sponsored outreaches, including *Lifeline*, a pro-life organization, *Lightline*, an anti-pornography league, and *Breakthrough*, World Harvest Church's daily and weekly television broadcast, currently heard by a potential audience of over 160 million people.

Pastor Rod Parsley also serves as Dr. Lester Sumrall's personal assistant in directing the End-Time Joseph "Feed The Hungry" program.

Additional copies of this book
are available from:

R E S U L T S

P U B L I S H I N G

World Harvest Church
P.O. Box 32932
Columbus, Ohio 43232

To contact Rod Parsley, you may
also write to the address above.
Please include your prayer
requests when you write